I Remember Papa
A Sicilian-American's Century

Mary Militano Winters

To Katherine
Enjoy all the old
memories of years
gone by, God Bless you,
Mary

DORRANCE PUBLISHING CO., INC.
PITTSBURGH, PENNSYLVANIA 15222

The contents of this work including, but not limited to, the accuracy of events, people, and places depicted; opinions expressed; permission to use previously published materials included; and any advice given or actions advocated are solely the responsibility of the author, who assumes all liability for said work and indemnifies the publisher against any claims stemming from publication of the work.

ISBN: 978-0-8059-7633-5
Library of Congress Control Number: 2007922615

Printed in the United States of America

First Printing

For more information or to order additional books, please contact:
Dorrance Publishing Co., Inc.
701 Smithfield Street
Third Floor
Pittsburgh, Pennsylvania 15222
U.S.A.
1-800-788-7654
www.dorrancebookstore.com

Dedication

I wrote this story because I wanted my family to appreciate what it was like to live in the United States, as the children of Sicilian immigrants, through the Great Depression and World War II. Don't let the name "Winters" fool you; my maiden name is "Accardo" and "Militano" is my first married name by my deceased husband, Joe. My parents and Joe's each are of direct Sicilian ancestry, with all four grandparents arriving in this great nation of ours by different means…yet ultimately of common cause and ancestry. As I prepared this text, I would enjoy bouncing memories of my childhood off my sister, Anna, whom we called "Nedu" as a child, and Kaye, who we called "Baby Kay." Anna was our little angel. We swore she was the real Fountain of Youth. Many years after Mama died, Anna took care of Papa and nurtured him along to a sturdy 105 years+ before Father Time called him up. "Baby Kaye" was the youngest and object of our fondest affections. Sadly, the scourge of cancer stole away our little angel, Anna, shortly before her seventy-ninth birthday, and Baby Kaye at seventy-seven. I dedicate this book to my wonderful sisters, Anna and Kaye, whose quick smiles and great spaghetti gravy we remember fondly and whom we shall miss until we meet again in a better place.

Contents

Acknowledgments

To my brother, Nick Accardo, who helped me locate old documents in my parent's safe, some written in Italian from Italy, some in English, documented in the United States.

To Victor DelPizzo, who, since my Italian language skills are rusty, helped me translate the Italian documents into English.

To Connie Caruso, my son Richard's wife, who taught me how to use the computer, a great personal breakthrough in itself, which enabled me to write this story.

To my sisters, Jeanette, Anna, and Kaye, who contributed invaluable memories.

And to my son, Joseph, who polished off his old newspaper editor's skills to wrap my fondest memories into a real story of hope and redemption.

Foreword

I Remember Papa is the story of Sicilian-American immigrants to the United States who endured some of the most tumultuous years of U.S. history. From the Great Depression through World War II, the sights, smells, and sounds of a Sicilian-American enclave in New Jersey come alive in the era of the trolley car and comedy radio shows. With the words of the song "Brother, Can You Spare a Dime?" ringing in his ears, future centenarian Jimmy Accardo experienced the irony of unemployment in the land of opportunity during the Depression, only to recover in time to see his only son and two sons-in-law go off to war. Throughout, the sounds of mandolin music playing in the streets, the sight of the family performing the Tarentella dance at backyard parties, and the smell of meatballs, sausage, and "gravy" are the one set of constants he could count on.

Prologue

It was August 30, 1887, when this "Papa" of ours was born in the town of Gibellina, in western Sicily, in the province of Trapani, southwest of Palermo. One century earlier, Gibellina was a center of research in classical archaeology. More than likely, Papa's father, Nunzio, didn't have much time for research. Nunzio Accardo, a thirty-six-year-old farmer domiciled in Gibellina, was a hard-working man given the eat-what-you-grow nature of western Sicily in those years. Vincenza Fontana, Papa's mother, gave birth to him at 10:23 a.m. at her house, located on Via Corso in Gibellina. You couldn't find the house today. In 1968, a massive earthquake destroyed many of the towns and villages of the Belice Valley, where Gibellina was located. What survived of the earthquake, and remained of the seventeenth century structures of this ancient Sicilian village, were ultimately demolished. Instead of rebuilding, a vast labyrinth cement work of art was erected to trace the paths and streets of the original village. Hence, today stands the Labyrinth of Gibellina, or *Cretto* in Italian, meaning the "crevice." While it was derided by many, at the time of its construction, the Labyrinth of Gibellina was the world's largest outdoor work of art.

This otherwise common, and relatively unremarkable, birth of Papa's nonetheless became an inception point for a future Sicilian-American family that navigated the waters of America and thrived for more than a century of his life. The event of Papa's birth was recorded for posterity and signed at the House of Commons in Gibellina by Antonio Gregorini, the secretary delegated by the mayor, who was the authorized official of the state for the village. Present as witnesses were Gregory Caltaldo, age forty-eight, and Calogero Cirello, age thirty-three, both farmers and residents of Gibellina. Neither could read nor write. They signed their names with an "X."

There is no record of Mama's birth. All that is known is that she was born in 1896 near the village of Trapani in Sicily. Well-documented records were a thing of luxury, to some extent, in the villages of western Sicily. If there were records at all, it would be difficult to authenticate the accuracy of the information.

Mama and Papa never met in the old country of Sicily. Had they remained, and never traveled to America, the odds are they would never have met. Villages tended to grow within themselves in Sicily. It would be an odd circumstance if they were to have ventured a few towns away. Connections were made through family. And there were plenty of family-made connections to go around in the close-knit quarters of a home village in Sicily.

Mama and Papa would take different routes to America, their land of promise. However, once in the New World, their paths would cross forever. They would live out the American Dream in ways that could never have been imagined in their little Sicilian villages. Instead, they would carry a slice of Sicily to America, and recreate in a dynamic new world a little of the old.

Chapter 1
Coming to America: The Early Years

Sulfur was one of the propulsion engines that powered the Industrial Revolution. The dynamic, flammable nature of sulfur led to numerous applications, not the least of which is gunpowder. It was, perhaps, both a blessing and a curse that sulfur was discovered in large quantities in Sicily centuries ago. Evidence suggests that as early as 900 B.C., the island's native peoples—Sicaniancs, Sicels, and Elymains—exported sulfur to Greece and North Africa. When the Industrial Revolution came exploding onto the European scene in the mid-eighteenth century, the British and the French in particular had new ideas for Sicily and its sulfur reserves. At one point, the British successfully negotiated exclusive contracts for Sicilian sulfur, which gave it a hammerlock on purchases. Soon, sulfur mining in Sicily reached international levels. By 1800, Sicily had a virtual monopoly on the western world's sulfur supply. In sulfur, the Sicilians had found much more than a natural resource that could generate much-needed revenue. Sulfur, in the broader sense, served and preserved the island's political prominence in an age of global military and industrial power.

Yet sulfur had left more than positive marks on Sicily. In many ways, it left scars too. The mines themselves were nightmarish environments. Deep and dangerous, the work was hard. The mines greatly contributed to an ecological "perfect storm" that systematically began to deforest and deteriorate the central Sicilian provinces. Powerful landholding institutions had sufficient resources to exploit vast territories to mine for sulfur. People and land were exploited for the gain of a few.

In the 1890s, a Roman Catholic priest, Father Luigi Sturzo, had seen enough. With a powerful brand of social activism, Father Sturzo organized miners to address head-on the inhumane working conditions and child exploitation brought on by the sulfur miners. Prompted by Pope Leo XIII's teachings about the role and responsibilities of labor, first Father Sturzo, and later the government of Italy, began to confront the sulfur mining establishment.

Father Sturzo would win, all right. Yet some of the costs were unanticipated. Until the turn of the century, in 1900, Sicily was the world's primary commercial source of sulfur-bearing compounds. Dozens of mines dotted the island. Soon, under intense political pressure, they would begin to disappear...one by one. In their wake, in many areas what was left behind was a ravaged, deforested land of beleaguered people. Mediocre agricultural policies and reckless exploitation had rendered food production inefficient. The Sicilian agrarians could barely produce enough food to sustain the island's growing population, much less expand the agriculture industry to replace the loss of the sulfur economy. By the turn of the century, much of Sicily had become a desperate place.

To say that many western Sicilians emigrated to America for a better life in the early twentieth century is an understatement of grand proportions. With the loss of its central sulfur economy, which had sustained it for centuries, and the agriculture industry unable to turn the tide, Sicily was poor. Prospects for the young were damp and gloomy, despite a warm, balmy climate, tremendous natural beauty, and a rich cultural heritage to enjoy. By the turn of the century, many of the island's unemployed, or underemployed youth, were in search of a better life. Of all the places on the planet, one stood out as the most promising of all. *America*.

By the age of twenty-nine, Papa was among a generation of young and restless Sicilians looking west for a better life. Compared to his prospects in Gibellina, America seemed like much more than a calculated risk to the Sicilians. Sicilian émigrés wrote back with stories of great advancement. Perhaps more importantly, America had proven itself relatively hospitable to the Sicilians. In itself, that was a big deal.

America's growing Sicilian population offered a bridge to this big and daunting new world. By 1916, more than two million Italians lived in the United States, many of them familgia to the fresh immigrants.

When Papa arrived at Ellis Island on November 22, 1916, he did what many Sicilian-Americans would do on their arrival in the United States. He went to live with relatives. He was processed on Ellis Island, and immediately went to live with the Venzas, of Newark, New Jersey. Newark had a huge Italian-American community, with a distinct Sicilian inflection. It was a regular starting point for the Sicilians emigrating to the United States.

On Papa's arrival, the Venzas somehow incorrectly translated his first name, Vincenzo, to "James," a simple mistake in translation. Yet, the seemingly minor error created the name of a young fellow new to America by the name of "Jimmy" Accardo. So much for Vincenzo. Barely in the country a few weeks, Papa's new country had given him a new name. Such abrupt and unceremonious name changes were nothing new to the immigrant Sicilians. Many misspelled their names at Ellis Island and the mistake would become theirs forever. Others simply "Americanized" their names to make life easier for them in the New World. As it was, Vincenzo Accardo of Gibellina, Sicily, would be instantly transformed into Jimmy Accardo of Newark, New Jersey. Ten years later, on September 30, 1926, he would become a naturalized American citizen.

Mama arrived in America before Papa, in 1899, when she was three years old, with her mother and father. She was the first child of Guiseppe Romano, "Nanu," and Maria Mendina, "Nana." Nanu had entered the seminary in Italy to become a priest. Yet somewhere along the line, Nanu decided that life as a priest was not his cup of tea. So he decided to leave the clergy. Soon, he was married, and on the way was the Romano's firstborn child, a baby daughter. She was named Antonina. She would be called "Lena." To us, she was Mama.

Early in their family life, Nanu and Nana had reached a crossroads of their own. Like Papa, and many other Sicilians, they too faced bleak economic prospects. They also received news that life was better for the Sicilians in America. Once their first son, Sam, had joined the family, the time had come to make a strategic decision. With great courage, and even greater expectations, they bundled up their daughter, Lena, and baby son, Sam, and boarded the Italian ship *The Prinzilai* and set sail for a better place in a new world—America.

Unlike most Italian émigrés, the Romanos would not pass beneath the welcoming salute of the Statue of Liberty before disembarkation in America. They would not travel the traditional route through New York harbor, to be processed on Ellis Island, where the vast majority of Italians would pour in. There, twelve million immigrants would enter the United States at a rate up to five thousand per day. Instead, the Romanos entered the United States in one of the next largest ports of entry before the turn of the century for Italian immigrants. It was a destination that emerged as a particular favorite of the warm-weathered, tropically-inclined Sicilians. With Mama and baby Sam in their tow, Nanu and Nana entered America through the sultry, southern port of New Orleans.

Once in America, the Romanos moved to the parish of Paterson in Livingston, Louisiana, where they lived for a while. Yet Nanu didn't take to the New Orleans surrounding area any better than he did the seminary. To him, the Irish immigrants there didn't like the Sicilians much. In his assessment, the Irish assumed the Sicilians were all connected to the Mafia in some way. Since many of the Irish were policeman, this wasn't a good thing at all, Nanu thought. Understanding Nanu's ethnic predicament, friends from up north wrote and told him to come to a place where the people were far more receptive to Sicilian immigrants. It was a state, in fact, where the Italians didn't feel like they were in the minority at all. Nanu was off again, this time settling in the "Italian section" of Union, in the village of Vauxhall, about twenty miles west of New York City, in the state of New Jersey.

A Meeting Not Left to Chance

How Mama and Papa first met, you might say, had not been a matter of love at first sight. The massive wave of immigration, and a twist of fate, had placed them in roughly the same geography. Yet from there, their meeting wasn't left to pure chance in the least. When Papa was in the U.S. and living with relatives, at the age of twenty-nine, by most Sicilian standards, he was growing too old to wait much longer before marrying and starting a family. Time would surely pass him by. So it wasn't very long before the family would be searching for a woman for him to marry. Having entered America as a relatively young man, the clock was running out nonetheless for Jimmy Accardo. He needed a wife—a nice Sicilian wife—before he got much older.

Mama told the story of the strange man sitting in the kitchen with her father, Nanu. She wasn't sure what this unfamiliar face was there for. Yet the conversation somehow seemed to strike home, literally. As they conversed, the tone became more and more serious. Maybe it was about a business deal? Or a job? Or about money? It never dawned on Mama that Vincenzo Accardo from Gibellina, Sicily, now Jimmy Accardo from Newark, New Jersey, was there for *her*. The Venzas were friends of Nanu's, and Papa was recommended as a fine young man. Papa must have done, or said, all the right things. Family recommendation or not, Papa could not offer for his daughter's hand in marriage had Papa failed this first impromptu Sicilian son-in-law examination. No doubt rattled by the experience, Papa soldiered through nonetheless. First, Papa would have to win Nanu's mind. Then, he would have to win Mama's heart. Before long, Mama and Papa were the product of a fairly common family occurrence among the new Sicilian immigrants to America. Their marriage, simply put, was "arranged."

At first, Mama resisted. She had another fellow in mind. Her eyes were on a young barber in town. Yet the man was a gambler. And Nanu's firstborn daughter would not be the wife of a gambler under any circumstances. Nanu would not consent. This would be a formidable force in any immigrant household, yet for the Sicilians it was much more damning. Mama continued to resist. Inevitably, her choice was to thumb her nose at her family's wishes or accept her fate. It was of no use. Under intense pressure, she relented. Now, Jimmy Accardo's marriage to Nanu's oldest daughter, Lena, was much more than just a matter of luck, or love at first site. Their marriage certificate reads April 28, 1917—the date when they went to City Hall in Newark to register. Yet, in terms of a family and faith, Mama and Papa were actually married on July 1, 1917, at St. Rocco's Roman Catholic Church in Newark, New Jersey. Years later, they would say that they got married first, and learned to love each other later.

In many respects, it wasn't surprising that Mama and Papa learned to love one another. Jimmy Accardo was a kind and decent man. He treated Mama with much love and respect. Mama was an equally kind and considerate woman. They would work hard together, to build a better world for one another. They were a product of *familgia*. And they would produce a family of their own. Together, theirs would be a rich, yet simple life, filled with children, grandchildren, music, wine, and great food. They would learn to love a country where they would learn to love each other as well.

Yet enough of the dates and facts. Very few people born in America found what Mama and Papa discovered together once they settled in this new world. Theirs is a wonderful story of life, new liberties, and the successful pursuit of happiness in a new world.

A New Life in a New World

Papa was a tall, thin man, with black wavy hair and hazel green eyes. He resembled George Burns in his senior years and occasionally even co-opted a few classic Burns' one-liners: Papa said he would never need a hearing aid...since he had heard it all before! Butta-bump! Mama was an attractive woman with light brown hair and an unusually light complexion, startling to some in America because of what they expected someone of Sicilian decent to look like. In reality, through centuries, Sicily had become a melting pot of its own, with many cultures having roots there. For years, Mama would wear a bun in her hair. The bun was a trademark for the simple life she had adopted. Ultimately, the bun had to be abandoned in America in favor of a "permanent." It took Mama's daughters, years later, to teach her how to put on makeup.

Living arrangements for the Accardo newlyweds was no more a matter of chance than the marriage itself. Mama and Papa lived in a flat upstairs from Mama's parent's home on Hilton Avenue in Vauxhall, a village within the town of Union, New Jersey, which bordered Springfield on the west, Maplewood to the east, and Millburn to the north. At the time, the area abounded with country farms. That suited Papa just fine, since it bore some resemblance to the old country in Sicily. There was no heat in the house except the little that could be generated by a wood-burning stove. Water was from an outdoor pump. The toilet was in the back yard in a small shed. It was called the ubiquitous "La Bachousa," Italian-American "pig Latin" for "back house." It was a quaint, light-hearted way to describe the outhouse in the back yard.

Papa came to the United States with a specific set of goals: To send money back to his parents in Sicily and, of course, to create a

6

better life for himself. Over the years, he sent money back to Sicily as often as he could. The Italian-Americans sent home an estimated $30 million per year before the Great Depression. Mama would send boxes of old clothing to the "relatives" in Sicily to help them out. While the Great Depression would eventually slow down the flow of money and used clothing to a mere trickle, Mama and Papa would still send something once in a while when they could afford it. They would never forget their roots.

Nicknames for Everybody!

Once in America, for the Romanos and Accardos renaming everyone was very important. Using Italian names could be counterproductive to assimilation. Nicknames, or Americanized names, suited the overall set of goals much better. One custom of Sicilian-American families was to name the firstborn son after the father of the bride or groom. Out of respect, Mama wanted to name their first son after Papa's father, Nunzio. So she sought out a derivation. A library clerk suggested "Newton." But that sounded far too "English" for Mama and was way overboard. So Mama decided to put the name "Nuncie" on the birth certificate, which, for a while at least, worked just fine. Yet even this well-thought-through name of "Nuncie" wouldn't last. Mama and Papa began to call Nuncie "NuNu." Then NuNu himself put the Americanized finishing touches on it, and referred to himself simply as "Nick." And so it would be. The second child, Vincenza, was called Jeanette. I was the third child, Maria. Somehow I was granted an accurate translation and spared the inevitable nickname. Surprisingly, for the Accardos, I was simply called Mary.

Mama's father, Nanu, was a mason and builder. Soon he built new homes for his family in Vauxhall, and another one for Mama and Papa. Theirs would be on a parcel of property adjacent to Nanu's backyard, well within Nanu's protective Sicilian sphere. It was a two-story, wood-framed house with a concrete basement, common in the Italian-American enclaves of New Jersey. The tall wood-frames were filled with the wonderful smells of homemade pasta sauce— "gravy" in Italian-American vernacular. Mandolin music would emanate from the narrow side alleys, only a couple of feet in width, which divided house from house and family from family. Large, attached wooden porches adorned the first and second decks of the houses in the rear yard.

Papa quickly turned his new home into a little slice of Sicily. The backyard was long and narrow with a concrete patio immediately at the base of the house. Behind the patio, Papa developed a wonderful grove loaded from end to end with fruits and vegetables. Coops for rabbits, who would soon meet their fate on the dinner table, next to the vino and pasta, stood there as well. The narrow yard was quickly converted into a mini-farm to create food for the family.

The new house was an overwhelming new wrung as Mama and Papa climbed their way up the social ladder of the American Dream. The house had all of the modern amenities: running water, a bathroom, and of course the biggest game-changer of all, electricity—thanks to Mr. Edison, the American hero of nearby Menlo Park, New Jersey. The gas lamps of the old house on Hilton Avenue gave way to the streetlights of the new house on Montclair Avenue. Dirt roads gave way to concrete. Although just a few blocks away by land, it was a world away in terms of the American Dream. Suddenly, Mama and Papa felt "rich." Everything seemed to be going exactly in the right direction, just as expected, in this new world of theirs in America.

A new house meant a new baby. Soon, Antonina would be born. The children, Jeanette and I, were shuttled next door to Nana's house on the big day to make room for the midwife and delivery. Across the narrow alleys, it was easy to hear all the noise and the sensation of the birth. The midwife moved the process along. Mama's moans became more and more pronounced. Soon, right on time, a new Antonina, named after Mama, was born. She would be called "Anna." It was cause for an instant celebration, Sicilian style! In the early morning hours, the spirit of the Old Country met the new in the narrow alleys between the homes of children and parents, where the sights and sounds of birth had just taken place. With a new baby in her arms, per custom, Mama was serenaded with music while in bed. As baby Anna cried, Mr. Louie, Papa's friend, along with his musician friends, performed a sweet ritual to welcome this little new person into the world…and to thank her mother for doing such a wonderful job with her pregnancy. For Mama to hear, Mr. Louie and his merry band of musicians were in the backyard, strumming their guitars and mandolins gently, serenading her wonderful human and family accomplishment. As Mama rested in bed, "Yes We Have No Bananas," a lively, musical expression of pure fun and joy, was being strummed in serenade to her by mandolin.

Of course, Anna had to have a nickname, which would be "NeDu." Now there was "Nanu," Mama's father; "Nana," Mama's mother; Mama was "DuNee;" "NuNu," their son, was Nick. Nobody ever got it straight. The short Sicilian nicknames drove the family crazy.

The Volstead Act

America may have been the land of opportunity for the Accardos. Yet there were peculiarities in some of the politics and thinking. Social conservatism was reaching a new zenith in 1920. Invariably, some of the trends would run counter to traditional Sicilian thinking. The Americans were not as enamored to gambling, at least on the surface. They didn't seem to have the same appetite for long suppers that would take the better part of an afternoon to consume. Yet with the passage by the United States Congress of the Volstead Act of 1920, America dealt a most serious blow to the Vauxhall Italian community. This time it was personal. It was an attack on one of the most fundamental aspects of Sicilian family culture—drinking wine.

The Eighteenth Amendment of the United States, the Volstead Act, was singularly ill-conceived. The intent versus the results could not have been more disastrous. The amendment prohibited the manufacture, distribution, and consumption of any drinking substance with more than .05 percent alcohol content. Having emigrated from a country where wine was as much a part of the family culture as pasta, the era of Prohibition now struck the Accardo family broadside. America was changing, all right. And it wasn't all for the better.

Nana's son, Uncle Leo, a local fireman, called Nana's house by telephone one day to say that the police department was going to pull off a raid in the neighborhood and not to be frightened. Apparently, the tenants at the Romano's rented house on Hilton Avenue were making "moonshine." The illegal whiskey had become a prime target of Prohibition-era raiders. To be sure, this was no Elliott Ness operation. These were small-town, local police. Their targets were hardly big-time thugs, or mobsters selling whiskey to a thirsty America. If anything, Prohibition gave rise to the Sicilian-led Mafia. Yet these were ordinary poor people, just having a nip here and there, trying to get by with a little "spirit" in their lives. Soon, the police were emptying barrel after barrel of mash over the rail of the tenant's upstairs porch into Nanu's garden down below. Their homemade booze flowed down Montclair Avenue for hours. The entire area smelled like whiskey for days.

Next door, in Nanu's cellar, the Sicilian uncles were hard at work. They would make homemade root beer. That was legal, of course. Yet it was hardly the main event. Vino was another matter altogether. Homemade wine was a staple. Virtually every Italian family in Vauxhall had a wine press, or some method of their own for making wine. For their part, the authorities didn't get involved much with personal consumption of beer and wine. In fact, a movement emerged in Washington, D.C., to permit at least that degree of tolerance. Yet for the Accardos, it didn't really matter much what the rules were when it came to vino. Nanu and the uncles quietly worked their wine presses with little concern for the law. Nothing was going to stop this Sicilian-American family from making the spirits that were central to the fabric of their lives. "Prohibition" or not, the vino would never stop flowing at Jimmy Accardo's Sicilian-American house in Vauxhall, New Jersey.

The American Dream Postponed: Tragedy Introduces Calamity
Mama and Papa's introduction into America, and the years that followed, would be typical of so many families emigrating to the United States in search of a better life. They would find friends, begin to raise their own families, and work hard to earn worldly possessions never dreamt of in the Old Country. Despite the hours of toil, all seemed to accrue wealth and happiness so gracefully and naturally in America. Yet soon the winds of change would spread like wildfire. With the grandeur of relative American "wealth" seemingly dead ahead, there would be little hint of what would come next. Yet as sure as an advancing storm, in the heady days of the "Roaring Twenties," things were about to change.

Next door to Mama and Papa's house on Montclair Avenue, Nanu and Nana were raising their other four children, Sam, Ben, Leo, and Catherine Romano. Indeed, the two families continued to grow. Soon, Mama was pregnant again. This time, a second Catherine was on the way, named after Mama's sister, Kay. Baby

Catherine was born a beautiful little girl with bright blonde hair and blue eyes. She wasted no time to demand attention—she developed whooping cough as an infant. This was no small ailment in the days before penicillin. In many cases, you either beat it or you died. Mama was determined to see the baby through it. She would walk Catherine up and down Montclair Avenue in her baby carriage. The doctors said the night air would clear up her throat. Yet, somehow, it just seemed that Catherine wasn't destined to do well in America, much less this fragile world, right from the start. Perhaps the whooping cough was an omen, which the Sicilians were always inclined to believe. Everything about Catherine seemed to be a struggle. There must be a reason.

Now with five children, ranging in age from six to ten, Mama and Papa had their hands full. There were the endless demands to stay on top of the hundreds of daily chores required to keep this growing and "modern" Sicilian-American household moving forward. Call it the pressures of the times, yet soon Mama and Papa began to fall prey to some of the inevitable shortcuts of parenting. There was just too much to do to stay on top of it all. And hard work, and overcoming obstacles, was central to the Accardo family culture. They were trying to get ahead in a new world. Yet, there wasn't enough time to get it all done. So juggling tasks, and using the older children to pitch in and help, became a family necessity. They would send the children on errands. They would give them work to do around the house. They would have one child watch the others. Even the family dog had a few tasks assigned. It was family automation in progress.

Fate, of course, doesn't herald its arrival. As Mama washed clothes one bright sunny day, she would take one such fateful short-cut. As the drone of the daily chores wore on, Mama scrubbed a mountain of clothes for the growing, seven-person family. She scrubbed on a small washboard in the kitchen sink. Sometimes the laundry had to be done early, before everyone returned home from work or school. Doing the laundry was particularly difficult, tedious, and physically exhausting work. Yet Mama scrubbed away, and plowed through the daily chores.

I was six years old when I was left alone to watch Baby Catherine on the second-story back porch. It was an ill-conceived mixture from the start. Part expedient, part necessary, part reckless—to Mama it was nothing more than a way to make it through the work day. From the second-story deck of the wood-framed house on Montclair Avenue, Baby Catherine lit up with a broad smile when she saw Grandma Nana approaching from the house next door. The baby stood up from her perch atop a wooden chair, braced herself against the second story balcony and beamed to see Nana. I didn't like what I saw at all. I called out to Mama, and pleaded with her to stop what she was doing to pull the baby down to safety and take the chair away. Yet fate had been tempted and was about to play its tragic hand. As Nana waved hello to the baby upstairs, Catherine leaned forward, smiled, and fell over the rail two stories to the concrete patio below.

Desperate, Mama bundled Baby Catherine in towels and rushed her, bleeding profusely in her arms, to Messner's pharmacy at the corner of Montclair Avenue. It was unrealistic to try to get an ambulance or a doctor to come to the house in an emergency during the 1920s in Vauxhall. There were very few telephones. So the most logical thing to do in an emergency was to run to the corner pharmacist, who would know as much as anyone what to do next. From Messner's, the police were called. Yet time was running out for poor Baby Catherine. As the sirens blared down Montclair Avenue, it was there in Messner's Pharmacy that beautiful little baby Catherine expired.

As tragedy struck the Accardo family of Vauxhall, New Jersey, the news media and police descended on the house on Montclair Avenue. Pictures of the tragedy would cover the front pages of the local newspapers. On the front page of *The Daily Mirror*, one of New Jersey's leading newspapers, there was a huge picture of the baby sitting in her high chair. She had a beautiful smile that seemed so out of context to her fate.

The holidays soon emerged but were hardly welcomed with joy. Sadness permeated the house on Montclair Avenue. With Christmas getting close, Mama and Papa concluded there should be no Christmas tree at all. There should be no celebration either. Instead, Mama could be heard crying every night from her bedroom. Having achieved so many firsts in America, and growing in wealth, the Accardo family now had a solid streak of sadness blended in. In many ways, it was a harbinger of things to come. For the first time since arriving in America, the Accardos were suddenly overwhelmed with feelings of strain and stress, just as America, itself, was about to plunge into an abyss.

On Christmas morning, 1928, the grief of Baby Catherine's death remained fresh to the Accardos. Yet the enchanted spirit of the day refused to be extinguished. Mama told the children that she hid each one of them a gift in a special spot somewhere in the house. The children had to go find them. The survivor's mentality had begun to burst through. There was a large, round oak table at one end of the living room. On top of it, in the center, was an old antique lamp that looked fascinating when it was lit. The round globe had an artistic base made from brass in the shape of trees. Beneath it was a green silk covering. The table had a massive center leg with three individual pedestals extended from it. From a child's perspective, it was a mountain of fascination.

With daylight emerging on Christmas morning, beneath this robust table, Mama hid the children's gifts. The girls were given pocketbooks as presents. Maybe they didn't have any money to put inside. No matter. The importance of having a few extra bucks had not yet dawned on the Accardos. The most important thing was there would be some semblance of a Christmas holiday for the Accardos after all. It was inevitable that this family of hardy immigrants would carry forward, tragedy or not. Christmas would help them rediscover the miracle of life.

Yet, omens and superstitions were something else altogether. If you were Sicilian, and if you looked hard enough for the signs, you could see just about anything coming in advance. Mama always talked about the huge black crow that would sit atop the clothesline pole in the backyard just before Baby Catherine's death. The bird appeared almost daily for a week before the accident. Mama was sure that it was a bad omen. She should have seen it coming. Then again, perhaps it was an omen of something else approaching, in some respects even more destructive and ominous.

Papa always blamed himself for the tragedy for not building the deck rail high enough. Mama blamed herself for leaving the baby alone. I blamed myself for not getting Mama to pay more attention. Papa built a much higher rail all around the back porch to protect the family. The higher rail would be one visible sign of emotional closure. It was a family grief that was strong, heartfelt, and enduring. Yet life was for the living for this hearty Sicilian-American family. Grief had its place. Then it was time to move on. It was part of longevity. Papa believed the family should have another child right away to compensate for the loss. So it would be. Within two years, a new baby "Catherine" arrived in the Accardo family. It was love at first sight. Unabashedly named after her predecessor, she would simply, and lovingly, be called "Baby Kaye."

Chapter 2
The Depression Years

Most women of Vauxhall, New Jersey, had a straightforward repertoire of clothing: a black dress for funerals, a silk dress for going out, and plenty of housedresses and aprons to work in with ugly black shoes. This work outfit suited Mama just fine. It was a house-wife's uniform of sorts.

Papa had to learn to read and write in English in order to work in the United States. There were many ethnic immigrants arriving in America, yet there were no signs posted in public places in their native language to help them get around. So the Sicilians felt com-pelled to learn how to speak English. The last thing anybody wanted to be in the still-growing, yet challenging economy of America was *unemployable*. So Papa attended class in a building provided for immi-grants located directly across the street from the Vauxhall Grammar School that the family attended. There, he learned to read and write in English.

Of course that didn't prevent Papa from reading his favorite Italian periodicals, especially the Italian newspaper *Il' Progresso*. Reading and writing soon became more than an occupational neces-sity for Papa in America. It became a way of staying connected to his roots, to keep in touch with life in the old country. He wrote letters to his parents in Sicily in Italian and was so happy when he received mail back from them. Correspondence with family in the Old Country was limited, given the relatively uncertain nature of the mail. Yet, the contact remained heartfelt nonetheless. One day, the mail would carry great news, such as the birth of a baby. Or, it would carry terrible news, such as the sad announcement of a death. One such letter arrived one day with sobering news for Papa. Via the mails, Papa learned of his own papa's death. Far removed from the old country by space and time, and unable to travel home, a cold, frustrating lament set in. So Papa created his own tribute to his father. He wore a black armband for weeks as a sign of respect and reflection.

For all the obstacles that Mama and Papa would overcome in America—from immigration through learning a new language, to raising a family and negotiating the uncertainties of a new country, to tragedy and death—few challenges could have been more unexpected for the Accardos in this "land of opportunity" than the one that was to follow. As the "Roaring" decade of the 1920s drew to a close, having been in the United States for well over a decade, Mama and Papa were now Americans, not just in the name or legal sense, yet in the sense that America had truly become their home. They were comfortable in America. They had friends and family, along with the certainty of support and consistency provided by the ethnic infrastructure that came from living in one of America's abundant and growing Italian-American enclaves, Vauxhall. They had come to the land of opportunity in America, and opportunity had come to them as expected. In real terms, America had saved the Accardos from economic calamity. Yet the economic conditions of the global economy didn't make exceptions for such ironies, which were about to unfold.

Despite the fact that the Accardos had come to America to find its fortunes, and ultimately did find them, the Great Depression arrived at the doorstep of 267 Montclair Avenue by the early 1930s, just as it did, somewhat unexpectedly, across all of America.

The American Dream Turned Upside-Down

Before the Great Depression, Papa worked for the Climax Crib Company in Newark, New Jersey. He was an expert at graining beds. He would often be sent to major hotels in New York City to set up beds and perform related tasks. It was a good job. Above all, it afforded a consistently improving lifestyle for the Accardo family.

For people such as the Accardos, who built their own houses, grew or hunted their own food, and made much of their own clothing, the word "economy" didn't mean very much to them in the late 1920s in America. The word had something to do with big companies, they figured. And the connection between the ultimate success of big companies and the daily fate of the Accardos seemed quite remote, if it existed at all. Yet, suddenly, like the abrupt thud of a hammer dropping on an anvil, the vortex of calamity began to suck the Accardos inside. Officially, the Great Depression struck on October 29, 1929, Black Tuesday, the day of the great Wall Street stock market crash. But for the Accardos, it was still someone else's problem. They could put food on the table without ever going to the supermarket. They could sew their own clothes. They could even build their own houses. The least of their worries was the stock market, since they never saw a share of stock in their lives.

Yet, the tidal wave of despair loomed closer then it seemed. Not too long after the crash, Papa, along with thirteen million American workers, fell into the chaotic straits of an imploding U.S. economy. As they say, a recession is when the other person loses their job; a depression is when you lose yours. Ultimately, Papa lost his job at Climax Crib. Now, the Great Depression struck home. The Accardos had gone from rags to riches in America. Now they were plummeting back down the ladder from riches to rags again.

Just before the Depression, Mama would happily buy clothes at The London Kiddy Shop in Newark. Now, minus a steady job for Papa, she could no longer afford to buy clothes. Instead, she had to sew all the clothes for the seven-person Accardo family. To make extra money, she took in sewing from a source in Newark for whom she would sew together certain articles. It wasn't easy work. It was boring. Yet it brought in some badly needed cash. When we girls arrived home from school, we would be expected to help with the sewing. Later at night, trying to do homework with fingers swollen from being accidentally poked with needles wasn't easy at all. Yet everyone had to pitch in to help Mama. No one complained. It was part of the Accardo family culture. And the Accardos, along with millions of Americans, were determined to survive the Great Depression.

Owning real estate was both a blessing and a curse for the Accardos during the Depression. The threat of foreclosure always loomed like a guillotine over our heads. Mama discovered a building and loan company in nearby Millburn, New Jersey, run by the Bunnel brothers, that helped out financially. To raise cash, Mama would go to the pawnbrokers in downtown Newark to hock jewelry. She had a beautiful cameo pin with a diamond that she hocked, and subsequently repurchased, several times. She hocked Papa's diamond stick pin. His cherished gold pocket watch and chain were always spared.

Then again, the house itself offered stability and, if lucky, a source of badly-needed cash. The house on Montclair Avenue was a two-family structure. To make money during the Depression, the first floor was rented out to help pay the mortgage. A sparsely furnished apartment on the second floor became home to the Accardos. The first-floor was rented to tenants, James and Christina Ricci, a nice Italian couple with lots of patience. They needed every bit of it to raise their five children in their small apartment, just like the Accardo landlords upstairs.

The Ricci's had a baby boy, Thomas, whom the first baby Catherine would play with all the time. Soon after Catherine's death, Thomas came down with pneumonia, another scourge of the era. When Thomas succumbed, superstitions immediately prevailed. Thomas's mother, Christina, was sure the two baby's deaths were connected. "Your baby called my baby to heaven," she surmised.

With the extra money from rent, Mama bought a small luxury, an Emerson Radio, and other items which the family needed to get by. Cash was tight, and the needs were great. Grandpa Nanu rented his first house on Hilton Avenue to bring in some extra money. Nana would go there to collect the rent once a month, but the poor African-American family who lived there were in tough straits themselves. They would fall two to three months behind in rent payments, once a full year. Nana couldn't speak English too well. So when she went to collect the rent, it never came out right. The family would get agitated, assuming she was insulting them in their misfortune. They would point their fists, and taunt her, until I corrected what Nana had said. In the end, the Accardos never had the heart to put the poor family out onto the streets. Cash was hard to come by. They would pay when they could. Or, they would find other ways to repay us. They would offer food or clothing as compensation. Everybody was in this Great Depression together, the Accardos thought. One good turn would generate another.

Depression Or Not...Sunday Dinner Must Go On!

267 Montclair Avenue was a vivid illustration of Sicilian-American life in the New Country. There were two large wine cellars with four or five barrels in each cellar. Papa stenciled roses on the wine cellar doors to add a touch of class. He would purchase large boxes of grapes. With the Great Depression making life difficult, and before he could afford a wine press, Papa had a method of his own for making wine. The grapes were thrown into the pit of one of the wine cellars in the basement, sometimes red, sometimes white. He used what he could get inexpensively and forged ahead. The specific type of grape, or wine, was secondary. To crush the grapes, Papa wore a pair of shoes with cleats on them. First, he stepped on and smashed the grapes. Then, he saved the juice by running it from a pipe nestled beneath a well in the concrete floor of the cellar. Below was a bucket to capture the juice. The well on the floor had a round lid cover on top of it so no one could accidentally fall into the pit below. Ingenious? Perhaps. Necessary? You bet. When it came to making homemade wine, any method was better than no method at all.

Ultimately, Papa purchased a wine press. It had a huge, circular wooden tub to crush the grapes in. It had a round lid over it with a large wooden handle that had to be turned and turned to squeeze out all the juice. There would be nothing left at the bottom but the grape skins, which could be used to make the more potent Grappa. Grandpa Nanu, who lived nextdoor, had a modern wine press. He was the greater expert in winemaking. Yet, sometimes a barrel of wine would turn sour and would taste like vinegar. So, in concert with the "no-waste" home culture of the Accardo family during the Depression, that is exactly what Mama used it for. Each barrel had a spigot. When the girls were told to go down and fill a bottle, we were warned to be extra careful not to leave the spigot leaking. That would mean big trouble with Papa. Wasted wine, dripping freely, was a major offense.

For all their needs, and with a limited ability to earn cash without the stability of a full-time job for either of them, one thing Mama and Papa had plenty of during the Depression was food. After all, these were resourceful Sicilians of farming ancestry. Fresh fruit, vegetables, and nuts from Papa's gardens, along with hunting and fishing, put food on the table. Papa grew a huge white walnut tree, taller than the two-story house, which was sufficiently huge to be featured in local newspapers. He grew peanuts. He planted several large fig trees, which he would wrap in linoleum during the winter months to prevent damage. The girls would climb the wild cherry tree after school in the summertime to feast on cherries. Grapevines wrapped around an arbor that resembled a shed. Under it was a huge navy hammock and a small table and chairs where Papa and his friends would play cards.

While President Herbert Hoover promised a "chicken in every pot," the Accardos were pretty much self-sufficient when it came to food. They certainly had no problem finding an eel or two for every pot. Eels were both easy to catch and a delicacy in many Sicilian households. You could do a lot with the eels. Papa would go fishing "down the shore" in New Jersey in the Barneget Bay. He would catch and bring home a basket of eels, dump them onto the concrete floor of the basement of the house on Montclair Avenue, and clean his dinner/prey. Each eel would be cut into four pieces. Then, into a huge pot of boiling gravy they would go. I was sure that the electric currents, common to the eels, made the pieces jump up and down in the boiling water.

Rabbits bred easily, which would make them worthwhile to raise in the coops in the backyard. We girls would be sent to the woods after school to pick grass to feed the rabbits. We knew better than to get too emotionally attached to the little critters. Ultimately, they wound up on the dinner table too, a fine *coniglio* dinner as Mama and Papa would call it in Italian.

During the Depression, Papa often went with his Italian friends to the woods nearby to pick mushrooms and dandelions. The dandelions were added to salads from the garden. The mushrooms were carefully picked over and fried with onions in a frying pan. They had their own unique way of testing whether the mushrooms were poisonous. They placed a quarter inside. If it turned black during the frying, that meant there was a bad mushroom in the mix that would potentially be poisonous. Of course, people could die eating poisoned mushrooms. When it happened, it would be the talk of Vauxhall for weeks. Yet, Papa knew from Sicily which mushrooms to pick. Apparently, he knew what he was doing. No one in the Accardo family ever got sick.

Even a *Great* Depression, or Prohibition for that matter, couldn't prevent the vino from flowing and pasta from being served at the

Accardo residence. Mama taught us girls how to make pasta when we were very young. She sat us down in two chairs facing each other with a large two-foot-by-two-foot pastry board on top of our laps. Next, Mama would place a large hunk of pasta dough on the board and demonstrate what shape of pasta to make. It was the most difficult to make tube pasta, hollow in the middle. The trick was to use a very strong, thin piece of wire about eight inches long. The goal was to take a small piece of dough and roll it around the wire until it formed a tube. Then we would carefully slide the tube of pasta from the wire and place it aside. Mama gently placed each pasta tube on a clean white cloth to dry out. To make gnocchi, Mama would take a one-inch long piece of dough and curl it up on the back of a pimply macaroni strainer with her thumb. The flat strainer would be used to shape the pasta into a small gnocchi. These were fairly easy to make. Yet the absolute easiest were the long, flat noodles, or "tagliatelli." So tagliatelli invariably was a staple. Making pasta by hand was tedious and tiring work. Yet no one could imagine Sunday dinner at the Accardo's without pasta, Depression, tedious work, or not.

Mama also taught the girls to make Italian cookies: Biscotti in different shapes and the Italian "filled" cookies. The filling was made from chopped chestnuts, prunes, raisins, or figs. The variations of fillings were left to our own taste buds. The tastiest and most difficult cookies to make were saved for holidays or special occasions.

In the summer, Nanu would make homemade ice cream. He had a large tub in which he packed dry ice. In the center was another tub in which he placed the ingredients for the ice cream. With the lid on, Nanu would churn the ingredients by turning the handle round and round until the liquid contents were frozen. The children would wait impatiently, literally with their tongues hanging out. Then, like a miracle, it was done. Everyone was served ice cream. Nanu beamed with pride at his accomplishment and the immediate effect that the ice cream had on the temperament of the children.

Of course, there were foods that couldn't be grown or raised and consequently had to be bought. Papa would travel to the center of Union to buy a one hundred-pound bag of potatoes for a dollar. The Sicilians were not expert potato growers. Since a one hundred-pound bag was much more than even a hearty seven-person family could eat before the potatoes spoiled, there was always the prospect of recouping some of the cost. Neighbors would buy a few pounds at the price of one cent per pound. For food products that they could not grow or catch, there was a "National" food store for items such as canned goods, flour, sugar, salt. Eggs were purchased from the African-American family who lived in the house behind the Accardos and raised chickens.

For all God-fearing Roman Catholic families, Friday night was "fish night." That didn't mean that the families ate only fish. The Sicilians, in fact, had plenty of options. They loved making "Pasta and Fajoli" (pasta with beans) or lentils and split pea soup. It was, perhaps, the most inexpensive way to feed a large family. Mama didn't always fit the stereotype and cook Italian food exclusively. She would often make a delicious roasted leg of lamb or a huge stuffed veal roast. There was a special option for the Accardo grandchildren. If any of the children didn't like what was being served in the Accardo house on Fridays, they could always go next door to Grandma Nana's house to see what she had cooked and eat there instead.

Sundays, holidays, and special occasions were times of great family celebrations. The food and drink were plentiful. The buffet at Nana's was loaded with marzipan fruit. Before a big holiday, the men would go hunting. There was never a shortage of great holiday meats. Above the china closet in Nana's dining room were reminders of the Accardo family's hunting tradition: There were stuffed pheasants that Uncle Ben had bagged. Nanu would skin rabbits in the basement; the little critters would hang from a rope extended from the ceiling. Then Nanu would cut a hole in the body and insert a wooden tube in the center. He would blow into the tube until the rabbit blew up like a balloon and the fur came away from the body. At just about that time, the children would run screaming from the basement.

When a holiday came around, there was a lot of cooking to be done. This was indeed a major project and all of the women were expected to help. All three kitchens—Mama's, Nana's, and Aunt Anna's (Uncle Sam's wife) across the street—would be in full operation. Together, they would create incredible feasts: turkey, pheasants, rabbits, lasagna, manicotti, spaghetti, sausage, meatballs, and pieces of pork cut up in the gravy. The fantastic smells of the pasta sauce, the "gravy," wafted throughout the house...and from house to house.

22

The Accardo family holiday dinners were always located at Nana's, per custom. Her huge dining room table would seat all the adults. An equally huge wooden kitchen table would seat all the children. It would not be unusual for holiday meals to last four to six hours. Time out between courses would be taken to loosen belts, maybe have a smoke, or play the piano.

Yet even while the Accardos feasted throughout the Great Depression, there were constant reminders that others were far less fortunate. Many people were miserably poor. Papa would occasionally catch someone trying to steal the family's milk, left at the doorstep by the milkman from Dvorin's Farms, one of the first dairy farms in Vauxhall. Papa would not confront the people. The culprit was simply poor and hungry. One such "thief" even sent the Accardos a pot of cooked beans, to reciprocate, when food conditions improved for him.

"No Waste" During the Depression

During the Great Depression, there was no such thing as "waste" in the Accardo household, especially when it came to food. In the fall, they picked tomatoes that didn't get a chance to ripen. Mama would simply fry them into a green tomato omelet with onions and maybe throw in an additional one or two red tomatoes. It was a scene out of the movie *Fried Green Tomatoes*, yet Mama's omelet was probably tastier. Papa raised tiny yellow tomatoes. So Mama found another recipe in the *Star Eagle* newspaper for "Yellow Tomato Preserves." It was wonderful, especially on the biscuits that Mama would make. One year, Papa had so many grapes from the vines in the backyard that Mama decided to make jam. She had a great recipe for "Heavenly Jam," and with help from us girls, Mama made enough to last for months.

It seemed nobody wasted food during the Great Depression. At the end of Montclair Avenue was a German bakery, named Faluchi's Bakery. It had a glass front display window to tempt passersby with all the pastry delights. Once per week, the Faluchis would take all of the leftover pastries, pound them back into a baking tray, and make huge sheets of what they dubbed "George Washington pies." They would ice the top of the recycled sheet cake with white icing and cut three-inch by three-inch squares. When we girls saw the George Washington pies in the window, we would run home and ask Mama for two cents to buy a single square. The Crystal Bakery nearby had a more traditional way of eliminating waste. They would simply reduce the price of day-old pastries by 50 percent.

In the 1930s, Rose & Rhienhold Rumstead's delicatessen was just around the corner from the house on Montclair Avenue, next to Tricarico's Chicken Market. The Rumsteads also emigrated to America, from Germany, for a better life. Mr. Rumstead was a professor of mathematics in the Old Country. Yet he was perfectly content in America with his delicatessen business. The Rumsteads were lovely people. They had their own way of dealing with potentially wasted food. They couldn't sell the hard and tough ends of the cold cuts that were formed into long tubes and sliced down. So when Mama would take the girls to the deli, Mr. Rumstead would give each of them a slice of cold cuts from the ends of the meats to eat while they waited. Such community pleasantries, and the Depression era "no waste" mentality, made food shopping with Mama fun...and tasty.

Mama's favorite butcher was "Bruno's." One might say Bruno specialized in "no waste": He was known for "sweetbreads" and tripe...which, in the Sicilian vernacular, consisted of cow's brains, lungs, kidneys, and stomachs. Of course, like many delicacies, the children couldn't stand to eat them. Mama and Papa couldn't get enough.

If any of the children had a job where food was created or served, it was expected that they bring some home. When Nunu was sixteen years old, he worked in a Jewish delicatessen a few blocks away in Maplewood. He would bring home the ends of the cold cuts that couldn't be sold or day-old fishcakes to be re-circulated for Friday dinner. Aunt Kaye worked in the Pastry Department of Bamberger's, the now defunct New Jersey department store ultimately folded into Macy's. She remembered everyone's birthday by bringing home a beautiful and delicious miniature birthday cake when it was their special day. The cake was about two inches in circumference and two inches high. Of course, it was never intended to be the main event. Mama always baked a large birthday cake for each member of the family.

In the midst of the Great Depression, even water was actively conserved. The water from the washing machine was run down into one of the washtubs in the basement and was reused to soak old rugs in. The clothes had to be sprinkled with water before they were ironed. To conserve water, Mama would use a Coca Cola bottle with a metal top with holes punched in it so the water would sprinkle out ever so lightly. Full reservoirs or not, nothing could be wasted during the Great Depression.

The Era of House Calls

As the Great Depression wore on, people became more and more resourceful when it came to ways to make money. If there was one thing you could still count on during the Great Depression, it was great service...brought directly to your own front door. Vendors peddling all kinds of wares would come directly to the house. The Accardos would get visits from the "Ice Man," the "Rag Man," the "Dry Goods Man," the "Junk Man," the "Bread Man," the "Italian Bread Man," and the "Banana Man." If you had a spare buck or two, you could even buy something from the "Fuller Brush Man."

The rag man was a particular Depression-era creation. He would literally live off rags. The sounds of the rag man, traveling by horse and wagon, would herald his arrival. The Accardos would sell their old rags for twenty-five cents, instead of keeping them for household chores. The "Dry Goods Man" came by bus with a large suitcase held on his back with shoulder straps. He would go directly to the back-yard to sell nightgowns, housedresses, aprons, and doilies. Fruits and vegetables were sold by the "Banana Man" off the back of a truck, with a scale fixed on the end for weighing the produce. House calls by doctors were expected. Going to the doctor's office was reserved for special needs. Dr. Renzulli would take the trolley down Springfield Avenue, lugging his big black bag alongside, to make house calls.

Of course, coal was delivered directly to the house. The coal was placed as close to its ultimate location of use as possible. The coal bin, approximately nine-feet by eight-feet, was located in the basement at the front of the house on Montclair Avenue. In order to receive the coal from a coal truck, an easily accessible window chute was required. The coal would be poured into the bin from the coal truck outside through a large metal chute. During the Great Depression, sometimes Papa would have to wait two or three days for delivery of the coal until he could scrape up enough money to pay for it.

Not surprisingly, the basement of the house at 267 Montclair Avenue, a prime storage location, had a distinct smell. In the winter, when the coal furnace was burning, the unique blend of wine from the barrels stored there, mixed with the smell of coal, created a special fragrance. In the winter, late in the evening, you could always find Papa down in the cellar, either fixing shoes or sifting through ashes from the bottom of the furnace, to salvage a few pieces of coal that could be reused to generate heat. Papa wasn't a shoemaker by trade, yet during the Depression he quickly learned how to repair shoes to save money. He kept a vice on the workbench and several iron shoe size forms. He bought new leather and heels and would hammer away. Sometimes, if it wasn't regulated correctly, a steam valve connected to the furnace in the basement would go off in the middle of the night. It made quite a racket throughout the house, a gonging sound much like a fire alarm. Suffice it to say, it wasn't very easy sleeping when one of the valves would go off and would clang all night long. Everyone got excited, and Papa would run down to the basement in the middle of the night, open the furnace door, and fix the valve, to stave off this nocturnal sleeping emergency.

The children played in the basement, especially in the winter, warmed by the heat of the furnace. Papa would paint pictures of birds on the cement block walls in lively colors to brighten the place up. Like many Depression era immigrants, the Accardos had few toys to play with. Brother Nunu built a scooter. There were a few pairs of roller skates, a jump rope, a ball, and a sled—a far cry from the Nintendo era. Summer months would provide simple modes of entertainment: catching fireflies in a jar, playing jump rope or teaming up to play the famously popular running game, "Red Rover, Red Rover."

In lieu of toys, Papa would simply create fun. He would throw pennies on a table and let the coins bounce around and hit the floor. The children scrambled for them. Call it allowance: Loaded with five cents, we could go to Mosby's, a "5 & 10" cent store on nearby Springfield Avenue, to buy a celluloid baby doll. Mama would leave scraps of fabric to make doll clothes with. Or the children would simply entertain each other. We girls would hoist our four-year-old sister, Baby Kaye, on to a chair and teach her to sing "The Object of My Affection." Affectionately, it became the baby's theme song.

In the evenings, the Accardos would go next door to visit grandpa and grandma Nana and Nanu to listen to the radio. In the early years of the Depression, a radio was well beyond Mama's and Papa's means. So it was a novelty to go next door to listen. It was the age of the radio shows—*Amos and Andy*, which was Nanu's favorite, and *Fibber Magee and Molly*—which were early radio versions of TV sitcoms. The Accardos would spend all night sipping vino, and eating cakes and cookies, while listening to the radio.

Homespun Medicine

Lots of folks had their own medical theories and played doctor during the Great Depression. Anything short of a serious injury had some type of homespun cure or remedy. It never really mattered whether the patient was immediately healed. Doctors were expensive and house calls were reserved for only the most intense medical scenarios. Somehow, it always felt better to be doing something rather than nothing at all, success or not. There were no flu shots, so invariably at least one member of the Accardo family would come down with the flu each year. Nana recommended a cold potato slice placed on the forehead for a fever. A high fever also meant a battle with the enema bag. For a sore throat, there was always the bottle of iodine. A long, wire-handled brush was used to swab the throat. After a trip to the beach, Mama would rub the children down with white vinegar if they were sunburned. Sometimes it seemed to work. Sometimes it didn't. To be sure, it didn't smell very good. Invariably, a modestly ill family member survived from whatever minor, temporary malady they endured. So no one ever questioned any of the so-called "remedies."

Some of the homespun medical remedies were better than others, in real terms. If someone had a chest cold, the jar of Vicks would be broken out, and the salve rubbed on the chests of the children. The overpowering scent would steal their breath away, and suddenly they could breathe again. There was castor oil and cod liver oil in liquid form for general good health. When Mama would come out with a tablespoon, poised for action, with one of the foul-smelling jars of oils in her hands, the children would scamper away and run and hide until the threat subsided. Papa was somehow always absolved from all of the bad-tasting stuff. While research has proven that some of those nasty oils indeed had medicinal benefits, Papa drew the line anyway. His excuse was that he didn't need any of the bad-tasting stuff since he ate plenty of sardines, either fresh or canned, drenched in healthy oils.

In general, Papa didn't care much for taking medicine, especially pills. He thought they were bad for you. It was probably a degree of Sicilian male pride, if not stubbornness. Yet he did make exceptions for aspirin. If he felt ill, an aspirin was about all that he would accept, in addition to a glass of vino, of course. In nearly every way, Papa was the picture of health. Few things would pull him under the weather. His eyesight, through the years, was another issue altogether. At one point, he badly needed a cataract operation. He relented, and unfortunately, it was not a success, no doubt further diminishing his confidence in the medical profession. He had to wear a frosted eyeglass on his left eye for the rest of his life, which he didn't appreciate very much. Yet Papa was still able to work, read, and write. The frosted eyeglass may have been a nuisance. Yet it didn't slow him down. When he couldn't find his eye cup, to wash out his bad eye, it wasn't a problem. He simply used a half walnut shell. Like everything else during the Great Depression, self-help for Jimmy Accardo remained the one thing you could always count on.

Busting Out with the Big Bands

For the Accardo children during the Great Depression, everything was harder to come by. Yet there were few, if any, emotional scars. Food was always on the table. There was always a roof over our heads. We were, after all, quite happy. We lived in a neighborhood with families of many different ethnic origins, which created a diverse and interesting community. The Stanley and Smith families were well-bred Gypsies. They had beautiful homes. This was so because they were not affected as much by the Great Depression as most people. In fact, you might say that the jobs of the Gypsies were "depression-proof." Speculation about the future during the Great Depression was in high demand. People wanted to know exactly where all of this was headed. So the Gypsy families would help them look ahead, if not with 100 percent accuracy, at least with a degree of unwarranted confidence. People would come from all over the area to get their palms read and project out their future paths with help from the Stanleys and the Smiths.

As a young woman, Wilhelmina Smith had a tent in Olympic Park in Irvington, New Jersey, a northern New Jersey hot-spot during the Depression. Olympic Park was a famous summer entertainment resort begun in 1887. It was the largest amusement park in New Jersey at the time. It was the perfect place for Wilhelmina Smith to set up a tent, telling fortunes from her crystal ball. She could tell you whether you would go from boom to bust and back to boom again.

Olympic Park was a favorite place for the Accardos, or any child or young adult in northern New Jersey during the Great Depression. It had a huge swimming pool, dozens of rides, including wood-framed roller coasters, and all types of food stands. Going to the park was like going on vacation. In many ways, it was a small respite that helped get the families through the Great Depression, adding a few perks along the road to recovery. Besides the movies, it was pretty much all that the Accardos, and other northern New Jersey families, had for entertainment. Mama would save tickets for the park that came from buying certain products. You could get a discount on food and rides, an important Depression-era consideration. The merry-go-round, one of the largest in the United States, was a favorite, especially since its organ was made in Italy and, as such, was a source of local Italian pride.

Olympic Park had a ballroom for dancing on Saturday nights where young adults could listen and dance to the famous orchestra of Paul Whiteman, his vocalist, Dolly Dawn, and other bands. Like many things during the Depression, the ballroom had multiple uses: it was used as well as an indoor rollerskating rink. There was a bandstand at the park where Dick Basile's band played every Sunday afternoon.

By the late 1930s and early 1940s, the "Big Bands" had arrived on the United States musical scene. The "jitterbug," a swing dance, was all the rage. Mama and Papa would allow us girls to roll up the rug in the parlor floor and put on records to learn the new dance. There was a lot at stake, much more than just impressing the boys. St. Joseph's Church in Maplewood would hold a yearly minstrel in which the girls would dance the jitterbug until the crowd went wild and demanded curtain calls. The girls would wear "Big Apple" skirts, which formed a full circle of fabric, so when they danced and swung it would flow all around them. They wore brown-and-white or black-and-white saddle shoes or penny loafers. A bobby pin would be strategically placed in the hair with a decoration of some sort on it. After a weekend of dancing, if Papa caught any of the girls still wearing lipstick or nail polish on Monday morning before school, he would make them remove it. That would be no way to go to school, which was serious business. It was where the Sicilian integration into American culture would take root, and wasn't to be messed with.

If Olympic Park wasn't on the agenda for fun, you could count on the Roman Catholic Church to throw a festival or two, a sure way to put smiles on the faces of the parishioners. Papa belonged to the Vauxhall section of St. Anthony's Fraternity in Union. Each year, on the feast of Saint Anthony, the Fraternity would conduct a huge, carnival-like festival. Occasionally, on Sunday, after mass at St. Joseph's Church, the men would carry a large statue of St. Anthony through the streets of Vauxhall. Some of the older Italian women marched barefoot, to atone for their sins in a gesture of penance. The people would come out into the streets to see the parade and pin money on the statue for charity. The Accardo girls would be dressed in their very best and lined the streets along with the other parishioners. When the statue of St. Anthony approached, they would be ready with dollar bills in their hands, a princely sum, to pin on the statue. The parade would ultimately wind up in St. Anthony's parking lot, where a band, perched atop a huge stage, played the most revered Italian songs loudly and proudly. Having completed their penance and charitable giving, now it was time for the parishioners to turn it up and have some fun. Arm-in-arm, the parishioners would link to dance to an Italian Tarentella. Carnival rides for the children whirled around. Stands with grills gave off the scent of fantastic Italian foods. The smell of Italian sausage and peppers wafted through the air blocks and blocks away, inviting the parishioners much like a scented version of the church bell. The priest would arrive to bless the loaves of bread. The Accardo girls were expected to eat some of the bread for good luck, not to mention the special blessing from St. Anthony that came with each bite. The festival was never completed until a huge fireworks display was put on at the end of the evening. Or, some unforeseen circumstance might dictate that the day was over, earlier than expected. One day, Papa spotted me walking around the carnival with a young boy. That was too much for Papa to tolerate. I was told to go home immediately, my feast terminated by a watchful Sicilian paternal eye.

Religion was central to the social fabric of Vauxhall. The entire village would be abuzz when Father Devine, the African-American Baptist Bible preacher, would come to visit. Born George Baker near

Savannah, Georgia, he began preaching in the South about 1900. In 1915, he moved to New York, where he founded the "Peace Mission Movement" and later adopted the name Father Devine. He would bring along his White Angel, a beautiful white woman entirely dressed in white. A stage was set outdoors a short distance from the Baptist church on Hilton Avenue. Folks would gather to hear the charismatic preacher do his thing. On Sundays, the parishioners of the Baptist church would have lively celebrations. Most of the women wore white clothes and would sing and shout, loudly and colorfully celebrating their religion. You could hear them singing blocks away. Religion played a unifying role in keeping the diverse Vauxhall community emotionally strung together during the Great Depression. From the Catholics to the Baptists, in Vauxhall, religion was both a source of pleasure and emotional comfort in otherwise stressful times.

Small Pleasures

While perks were few and far between during the Great Depression, Mama and Papa made sure they enjoyed small pleasures. Perhaps as a way of staring down the elusiveness of wealth, Mama would buy Papa only the distinctive Gold Toe socks. For herself, she would buy Daniel Green slippers. Papa liked Old Spice aftershave. Mama liked Lilac cologne and Coty's Air Spun Powder, face powder that was supposed to give ordinary women the matte skin of silver screen movie stars. Mama and Papa lived and died for Bamberger's, the New Jersey department store long since sold to Macy's, which was their favorite. If you gave them a gift of any other brand, odds were Mama would simply return it and go to Bamberger's to get what she really wanted anyway. Papa could always relax by smoking one of his favorite cigars, the extra strong Di Napolis or Marconis. They smelled terrible and Mama would always yell at him to go outside on the back porch to smoke. Yet old habits, especially enjoyable ones, died hard. The smell inside the house got much better when Papa began to smoke a pipe.

Mama loved the movies. Papa could care less. She adored Al Olson in the smash hit movie, *The Singing Fool*, and its hit theme song, "Sonny Boy," the first one-million record seller. It was one of Mama's favorite songs and filled the airwaves. On Saturdays, we girls were given ten cents each to go to the movies as allowance for housework. Sometimes, Uncle Leo, the fireman, would give us each one dollar when he was paid, a princely sum of money. After cleaning the house, we would walk to the Maplewood Theatre about two miles from the house on Montclair Avenue. Sometimes, it was easier walking to the movies then it was walking back home late at night. That was the case after one of the new-wave monster movies: *Frankenstein*, starring Boris Karloff, Bella Lugosi as "Dracula," or Lon Chaney, Jr., as the "Wolfman." On those evenings, sleep would be hard to come by.

Instead of going to the movies, sometimes the girls might use their money for trolley-car fare up Springfield Avenue in Maplewood and Newark to go shopping. In the summer, the trolleys were kept open; the sides had only metal frames with screening. There were hazards with this: on one occasion when it rained, I was caught wearing a crepe dress that immediately shrunk. Suffice it to say, I was ashamed to get off the trolley all soaked and wearing a suddenly form-fitting dress.

Mama's subscribed to *The Liberty Magazine*, which cost five cents per copy, and contained a wide variety of information on a range of topics. For her, it was another Depression-era perk. Mama loved to read. A huge doctor's book, printed in the 1920's, which she often referred to when needed, contained sage advice for pregnant women: "When you start getting labor pains, call for the horse and buggy!" The girls got lessons of their own from the old, beat-up doctor's book. If Mama caught anyone gawking at pictures of the male anatomy and giggling, she would take the book away.

The Accardos could not afford to have a newspaper delivered to their house. So the only way they learned about "breaking news" was by someone selling newspapers on the main streets hollering, "Extra, extra." That's how they would learn about the biggest stories of the era, such as the day when calamity struck the first transatlantic aircraft flier, New Jersey's own Charles Lindbergh of the famed *Spirit of St. Louis*, when his baby was kidnapped. Or in 1934 when the luxury cruise ship, *Morro Castle*, ran aground "down the shore" at Asbury Park, New Jersey.

Without a car during the Depression, on Sundays the Accardos often enjoyed the good life by hiking up to nearby South Mountain Reservation, a huge, two thousand-acre wooded reserve of hills and streams and walking trails. South Mountain provided a unique retreat from New Jersey's already growing and congested suburbia. All of it reminded Papa of growing up in Sicily, with its beautiful green hillside foliage. On clear days from South Mountain, you could see the bridges and buildings of New York City, just twenty miles to the east, yet a world away in terms of settings.

Papa taught the girls to climb up the face of nearby Eagle Rock Mountain. This was no small task. Eagle Rock was steep and not always so forgiving. Papa understood that all too well. He was especially careful. One year, a ten-year-old girl fell off the cliff and was killed. Her body was displayed in the living room of her nearby house in Vauxhall. The tragedy served as a reminder to the Accardos to be careful while hiking.

The Accardo family had wonderful picnics at South Mountain Reservation. Papa's friend, Mr. Louie, or Uncle Sam would occasionally drive the family up by car, a novelty in itself. Mama and the other women would bring lots of great food. The smell of Papa's sausage would travel through the air and attract admirers hungry for a taste. The water from the streams was perfectly pure, a special treat, so Papa would bottle some and bring it home. A watermelon would be placed in the stream to keep it cool before it was eaten. Trips to South Mountain ended with a brick of ice cream from Messner's drug store at the top of Montclair Avenue. It would be the perfect ending to a perfect day.

As the girls grew older, South Mountain would serve a different set of purposes. Far away from the watchful eyes of Mama and Papa, we would chip in with girlfriends to buy a pack of cigarettes. Once atop South Mountain, we would retreat into a cozy log cabin gazebo, with wooden seats around it, which afforded a gorgeous view of the valley and all of the nearby towns below. Safely hidden inside the Summer House, we "learned" to smoke. My best friend, Louise Petruzziello, would be terrified that we might get caught. But learn to smoke we did.

The top-of-the-line vacation for the Accardos during the Great Depression was going to the Jersey Shore with the Loria family.

Keansburg. Asbury Park. Atlantic City. All had great boardwalks with rides and concessions for the children. Typically, there were no reservations made in advance. Instead, the two families would find a small bungalow, presumably intended for a single family, and crowd everybody into it. There were three beds for more than ten people: one bed for Mr. and Mrs. Loria, one for Mama and Papa, and one bed for all the kids! That bed was turned sideways so the little ones could lay head-to-toe across the narrow part of the bed, to fit the maximum number of children. Only the couch and floor remained for the unlucky ones who didn't grab a spot. In the morning, the family members would sneak out to the beach, one by one, so the landlord didn't notice that two families were staying in the bungalow instead of one.

Pastimes during the Great Depression were sometimes inherited. One person's misfortune might turn out to be another person's fortune. An old German tenant, who was renting an apartment in the Accardo house on Montclair Avenue, was suddenly unable to pay the rent. So he gave Papa a radio instead, since the Accardos could not afford a new one. This was big deal, indeed. The old German man taught brother Nick how the radio was operated and how to hook it up. Nick, who would go on to be an engineer, kept it in working condition. Papa had the radio built into the top of a desk. A six-volt car battery in the lower compartment of the desk kept the radio working. A speaker on top of the desk broadcasted the sound. The antenna wire was strung inside around the room and then went to the clothesline pole outside, and nearly fifty feet away, for better transmission. While it could only receive A.M. radio, it could access stations from Newark, New York City, and once in a while all the way from Chicago. When boxing matches were broadcast on the radio, Papa invited all the men from the neighborhood to the house to listen. Whether the fighter was Gene Tunney or Max Baer, one thing was certain: it was impossible for the children to fall asleep until the fights were over. Only then would the men stop yelling wildly and go home.

For all of the little "perks," the real Accardo largesse during the Great Depression was securely placed inside a large, special trunk that Mama kept in her bedroom. Inside were the many Accardo family "fine items," including delicate, beautiful lace. The treasure chest included Nana's old wedding gown, a light blue taffeta. While these were family treasures, they could not go unused. Everything had to have an active purpose. Mama let me wear the wedding dress one year to a costume party.

For Papa, there were few pleasures greater in life than playing cards. Pinochle was a particular Sicilian favorite. Papa and his cronies would gather around a huge dining room table and shuffle the cards. They played for nickels and dimes for hours and hours, yelling and screaming when somebody drew a particularly good hand. In cards, practice did make perfect. And Papa spent many hours practicing. Papa and his partner would come up the winners at an above-normal rate, which ultimately made the other men mad. Years later, the sons-in-law were drafted into the games. Papa would keep the family tradition alive and teach them pinochle—for money, of course. He would walk to the Militano's house in Maplewood for a round. If someone had to quit, they would summon one of the children. Twelve-year-old Frank Militano, who was called "Babe," learned the game simply by watching. With all these howling men, sometimes it was fun for Babe, other times it wasn't. If he didn't want to be drafted into the game after coming home from school, Babe would simply go and hide.

For all the various things the Accardos did to enjoy life during the Depression, ultimately it was their resourcefulness that kept them positively focused, physically and emotionally. In some ways, symbolic of Papa's resourcefulness was a simple pocket knife, his favorite piece of equipment, which he carried his entire life. He was never without it—it was like a little treasure to him. It came in handy in the garden. It came in handy when the children wanted a piece of fruit cut in half. It came in handy when a walking stick had to be whittled for weekend hikes. Anna once saw him cut his toenails with it. Like the pocket knife, Papa was simple and resourceful. The Great Depression would test both traits, and when it was all over, Papa was stronger and happier than ever.

Cleaning the House

The Great Depression was a supreme test of America's mettle and resolve, and the Accardo's too. Relatively, they were far better off than most people, even those who lived in apartments, or "cold-water flats," as they were called. There was plenty of food, and their luck never ran out in terms of fighting foreclosure on the two-family house on Montclair Avenue. Yet owning a home also meant there were plenty of chores to do. And the Accardos were fairly pragmatic when it came to spreading the household work around. Male or female. Young or old. It didn't matter very much. There was work to be done. It would be unconscionable to leave it all to Mama and Papa. Cleaning the house wasn't work for women or men. It was work for the entire family. The girls got most of the "feminine" work inside the house, while Papa and Nunu did the "men's" chores outside. It seemed like a reasonable division of labor.

Everyone was expected to pitch in, no questions asked. Even the dog, Jackie, a short-haired, black-and-white male, was a beast of burden. Mama would often send Jackie to fetch the children when she needed them if they were playing somewhere in the neighborhood, or if the girls were gone too long at the corner stores. Mama would send Jackie to sniff his way to the girls and soon he would return home, with the girls not far behind.

The Accardos had tremendous pride when it came to keeping a clean house. Sometimes, it even got a bit compulsive, as if there was something to prove. Once per month, Mama would take down all the food canisters in the kitchen. They were made of china and sat atop the kitchen cupboard. The dry foodstuff inside, such as pasta, for the most part didn't need to be disturbed. Nonetheless, Mama directed that the canisters had to be washed inside and out. The contents of every canister had to be emptied into a bowl. Once the canisters had been washed, they would be refilled and placed back atop the cupboard. It was meaningless and unnecessary work. Yet there was a point: the Accardos would never compromise on cleanliness. Great Depression or not, the house on Montclair Avenue would always be clean. It would be well-stocked with food, and the children would be properly dressed and respectful.

Mama was particularly fussy. When the girls cleaned a bedroom, the bed had to be moved away from the wall and all the moldings in the room had to be scrubbed down. They would do the same and clean behind the piano. There could be no spots that fell to prey to dirtiness. During the Depression, for the Accardos scrubbing spelled redemption.

With five children, clothes were washed every single day. Barely five years old, my job was to stand on a kitchen chair and scrub clothes on an old iron washboard with Octagon soap. It was harder than it sounds, especially for a five-year-old. Mama and Nana would buy the Octagon soap powders with coupons from the products they bought. The soap smelled particularly foul. Yet there was an upside to the whole process: there were enough coupons to purchase treats. Mama would save as many coupons as she could until Christmas and would then redeem them to buy the girls baby dolls. The dolls would not come as much of a surprise: the children knew exactly where Mama would hide them—in Nana's closet.

Ultimately, Mama and Papa bought an electric washing machine, a Maytag. It had a large tub for washing and above it were double rollers to run the clothes through to squeeze out the water. The new machine brought occupational hazards: Mama and the girls had to be careful not to catch their fingers in the rollers when feeding in the wet clothes. The girls were extra careful to not catch the sleeves of their clothes in the spin dryer. Stories abounded of women suffering serious injuries from washing machine accidents. One woman caught her hair in the rollers. Others caught their hands. Another woman was even less fortunate: word was that she caught her breast in the dryer!

Mama's second washing machine came with a perk: it was an Easy Spin Dryer that had a spinner basket on the side. The clothes went from the washer directly to the spin dryer. Papa created other amenities. Mama had arthritis so Papa didn't want her doing laundry on the cold concrete floor of the basement. So, he built a wooden platform below the two wash tubs. While the girls were taught how to help with the laundry, neither Papa nor Nunu learned how to operate the washing machine. Doing laundry definitely could not be expected of a Sicilian husband, or son.

In such a neat-conscious household, everything was ironed: pillowcases, sheets, tablecloths...anything that could wrinkle. Nana taught the girls how to iron men's shirts. Before electricity, the heavy metal iron itself had to be heated on top of the stove. Following a laborious ironing session, Nana would give us girls a hot lunch that included a glass of red wine. Nana thought the ironing wore the children down and the wine would rebuild our strength. Forget about the fact that the wine got us a tad dizzy. Nana said we had to drink it to build our blood back up after the exhausting work.

Most of the windows in the house had lace curtains. When they were washed, they were usually hung to dry outdoors, weather permitting, on wood-frame stretchers. The frames had pins on the wood approximately two inches apart on which the sheer lace curtains would be attached to dry. The frames were set up in the backyard in the sun. Once the curtains were dried, the frames had to be taken apart and put away until the next time they were used. Two clotheslines stretched from the house to a pole in the backyard. It was a system that worked. When the clothes were pulled in, the clothespins were saved in a bag hanging from the end of the fixture that held the clothesline. Reeling in the clothes from the line was easier said than done. It took some muscle and was hard work for the young girls. It was especially hard work for me, even in my teens, under one hundred pounds and skinny. Yet the clothes smelled so clean and refreshing when they were pulled back in after drying in the fresh air. It was a special treat to wear them.

Pests made housecleaning extra hard during the Depression. In 1934, many parlor chairs were made of mohair or a sort of velvety texture that often became infested with moths. The moths would eat away at the parlor chairs, which ultimately made them look ratty. It happened to pretty much everyone, even the very cleanest of people. Essentially, people learned to live with the moths until they could afford to buy new living room chairs. Once the furniture industry began to use modern fabrics, including tapestry or silk, the problem was solved.

Many homes put out grass rugs in the summertime and slipcovers over the parlor chairs to make them cooler. Since there was no air conditioning, window draperies were removed in the summer in favor of light-weight summer curtains, to keep a cool breeze flowing in. When winter rolled around, it was time to remove the slipcovers on the chairs, wash them, and save them. Then, Mama and Papa would roll up the grass rugs and put back down a more substantial winter rug.

Every spring, Nana would take the bed pillows outside and empty all the feathers into a tub to wash the covers. Once the pillow covers were clean, she would put the feathers back inside. Mattresses, which were stuffed with goose feathers, had to be plumped up every night before bedtime. Bedbugs would lodge inside the springs so Nana would spray disinfectant. The girls hated that work; the bedbugs would fall to the floor. It was a nasty race to step on the survivors before they got away. Mattresses seemed to contain all kinds of pests. About once per month in grammar school, the nurse would come in and line up the children to examine everyone's head for lice. Papa bought new mattresses to escape such infestation.

Along with an unending ability to put food on the table during the Great Depression, the Accardo family pride centered around keeping a clean house. Like hunting, or growing and gathering food, house-cleaning was a family project. In many respects, housecleaning was a uniting force that pulled the family together in what was perhaps the most calamitous time of U.S. history.

Women's Jobs/Men's Jobs

By the time of the Great Depression, Nanu's son, Uncle Sam, was married. Nanu had built Sam a beautiful house across the street on Montclair Avenue. The concrete front porch had huge cement lions heads on each side of the steps for ornaments. Gorgeous chandeliers hung from the dining room and living room, which also had a magnif-icent fireplace. When times got tough, Uncle Sam started a business in his basement and raised enough cash to keep the house.

Uncle Sam and Aunt Anna had two daughters, Maryann and Betty. They were natural play-pals for the Accardo girls. They were more than neighbors. They were of the highest caliber...*family*. Maryann was a wonderful pianist who was awarded a scholarship to The Julliard School. Yet the thought of one of the girls going to school in New York City was still a little a bit overwhelming for this immi-grant Sicilian family. It was simply out of the question. It was way too far outside of the protective zone of the Italian-American enclave in which the Romanos and Accardos lived in Vauxhall, especially for a female. Uncle Sam simply would not permit it.

The uncles next door, on the other hand, had varied professions. Uncle Ben was a prominent lawyer who later successfully entered local politics. Uncle Leo was a Union, New Jersey, Fire Department captain. Uncle Sam had a business refinishing radiator covers, with specialty decorating, which he performed from the basement of his home.

It was understood from the start that Nunu, the only Accardo boy, would go to college. He would pick a profession that was sure to earn money. He attended the evening division of the Newark College of Engineering. To get to school, he bought a car, a Whippet, for five dollars.

The Accardo girls, on the other hand, were expected to go to work or get married—or both. Going to college for the girls, on the limited Accardo family income, was simply out of the question. Papa wanted me to become a beautician since I always did Mama's hair and was good at it. Instead, I became an executive secretary, at the time mostly "women's work." My ultimate dream was to open up a dress shop with Tina Militano, who years later would become my sister-in-law. Tina was an excellent seamstress and had great taste in fashion. While in grammar school during the summer vacation months, I would pass the time drawing fashions. Yet, somehow opening a dress shop seemed equally unattainable as going to college. Each would cost money, something the Accardos had very little of.

It was not unusual for an American family during the early part of the twentieth century to divide everything, from household chores to the quality of education, based on gender. The Accardos didn't think much about it. We simply saw it as a way of life.

An End of an Era

Sicilian-Americans were particularly susceptible to interference from La Cosa Nostra during the Great Depression. With money so tight, and Prohibition from 1920 to 1933 aimed at preventing people from having a nip of wine or spirits on occasion, things began to change. The Mafia began to thrive in America. Selling booze under the table became an illegal industry, turning the law on its ear. A gangster family in Chicago, known as the "Accardis," invariably led to questions about the "Accardo" family of Vauxhall, New Jersey. When the former made headlines, the Accardo children were asked at school if they were related to the "mob Accardis." Of course the answer was no, but the school kids weren't buying it very much. Even though they were the Accardos, not the Accardis, the suspicion never seemed to melt away. Maybe it was simply what people wanted to believe. If you were Sicilian, somehow, somewhere, you were probably connected to the mob.

One day, as the Accardo children arrived home from school, they found a strange man visiting the house on Montclair Avenue. Mama told the children to stay out of the parlor and keep quiet above all else. She would explain later. It was obvious that Papa didn't know the man very well. He was an acquaintance of some nature. Yet, they were both Sicilian immigrants, with common friends back in the "old country." So there were certain expectations. It seemed the strange man was in trouble with the law in Long Branch, New Jersey. He asked Papa to hide him at the house on Montclair Avenue for several weeks until the "coast was cleared." Papa was afraid. He didn't want any trouble. Turning the man down might ultimately backfire. Papa especially didn't want anything in return. At a minimum, he did not want the man beholden to him, which could create an endless stream of trouble. So Papa told the man he could stay in the house for only two weeks. Then he would have to go and never come back again. It was an honorable and reasonable proposition, and one that the man could not refuse in good faith. That would be a gesture of disrespect in itself, and wouldn't be tolerated. By the standards of the Sicilian community, he would be considered a thug. So he complied. When the two-week span was up, the strange man departed. He offered to give Papa a new automobile for harboring him. But Papa wanted nothing to do with the man anymore. All he wanted was to have the man leave as quickly as possible. No automobile, or any other gift, would be necessary. Such a gift would have symbolic value that would only encourage future transgressions.

In this small example, the mystery of the Mafia in the late 1930s was both confirmed and refuted. Of course the mob existed. Yet the notion that it somehow had a stranglehold on the Sicilian immigrants was rejected by a simple man named Jimmy Accardo, and everyday people just like him. Even though Papa had no money to purchase a car of his own, and was always picked up by someone to go to work, he never considered accepting the "gift" from the stranger. Papa was an honest man. Even the needs and demands of the Great Depression could not corrupt him. When it came to a free car, if it was of ill-gotten gains, for Papa it was nothing doing.

By the time President Roosevelt began the first of his twenty-seven famous radio "Fireside Chats," the first American presidential broadcasts, Papa badly needed a job. Beginning with the now traditional salutation, "my fellow Americans," the broadcasts, typically on Sunday evenings at first, had become mandatory listening in the

Italian section of Vauxhall. Soon, President Roosevelt led passage of the National Recovery Act. The Workmens' Project Administration, or WPA, was formed to put America back to work. The Civilian Conservation Corp, or CCC, paid one dollar per day. That was plenty fair to Papa. With the hit song, "Brother, Can You Spare a Dime?" ringing in his ears, Papa signed up with the WPA at the Municipal Building in Union. For the next few years, the U.S government, through the WPA, would become Papa's new employer. It was excruciatingly hard work. The men were tasked with all kinds of municipal clean-up and repair jobs. Papa would come home dirty and tired but would never complain about digging ditches, or the pay. He just accepted whatever work he could get. After all, it was work, something he hadn't had for a long time. It restored pride. Papa was more than happy to have a job, any job.

A government inspector, Sadie Sachs, would come to the Accardo house at Montclair Avenue once per week to make sure the family really was in need, and not exaggerating their condition. She was a nice lady. It was her job to ensure that the government largesse and real family needs were kept in balance and nobody was fudging. Sometimes she would bring shoes for the family. She would send Papa into town for an allotment of meat cured by salt, the only realistic method of preserving the meat.

Day-by-day, little-by-little, with the return of work, the Great Depression began to subside for the Accardos. The U.S. economy slowly crept back to life as well. Good times began to return to Vauxhall. The "land of opportunity" was beginning to live up to its reputation once again. Finally, as the Depression melted away, Papa got a regular job as a house painter. In the 1940s, many of the living and dining room walls of houses had in-laid panels. Papa put his down-home ingeniousness to work. He devised a special way of using paint to brighten up the atmosphere. He would highlight the rooms by painting the in-laid sections of the panels a deeper shade than the walls. Then with a sponge he made imprints that formed a beautiful design. He would also grain the woodwork trim in each room to resemble real wood graining. Papa saw his work as a creation of art. And his customers adored what he created.

Yet painting was difficult work. It wasn't always creative. Sometimes it was pure work...and risk. It certainly wasn't all about painting walls. One day, Papa and his fellow workers were painting a church in downtown Newark. The workers were wary of painting the steeple, which soared high above the church. It was dangerous. But the determination of this newly employed generation of American workers could not be underestimated. Papa didn't necessarily see it as a challenge. He simply knew it had to be painted. It was part of the job. And Papa was thankful to have a job. If the Depression and joblessness didn't strike fear in his heart, no steeple would. Up he went and finished the job.

As the Depression gradually drew to a close, Mama went to work at the Plastic Laminating Co. on Springfield Avenue, about ten minutes walking distance from the house on Montclair Avenue. That meant we girls were expected to pick up even more of the household chores. We were expected to start dinner when we arrived home from school, before Mama returned from work. Mama loved her job and often told us girls all about her work. She too had pride in workmanship. The job had its perks. Mama would bring photos from home to laminate on the board that she was working on. As long as the boss approved, and there was enough room left on the board, she could laminate her personal photos.

The children had jobs too. After high school, we would go to work in various low-wage positions. Yet for us there was a twist: we would be required to give Mama and Papa our pay, which wasn't much to begin with. Mama would give the children ten dollars back for lunch and car fare. If we children needed extra money to buy clothing, Mama would let us keep the money we earned. Sometimes she even added to the sum. Yet in the end, family needs always overruled.

At the age of sixteen, having graduated from high school, I couldn't find a job. Everywhere I applied, they suggested I go back to school to get a college degree. But that was out of the question for one of the female members of the Accardo family. But I kept pressing for a job. Soon, I was hired by Bamberger's department store in Newark, working at the refund desk in the basement. Determined to somehow get ahead, and with the Depression now a recent memory, I began to study shorthand and typing each night at the old wooden desk inherited from Uncle Ben. When I achieved my goal of being named secretary to one of the Vice Presidents at Bamberger's, Mama and Papa beamed with pride. Secretarial and administrative work was considered top of the line for a female.

With the Depression fading away, the Accardos were now fully employed. So they began to flex their newfound financial muscles. Now, they were able to buy nice furniture once again. Mama could buy clothes from Bamberger's in Newark. Weddings became a time to show the family "wealth" just a bit. When the oldest Accardo daughter, Jeanette, was married in 1941, Mama bought a beautiful flowered hat and blue lace dress. She made up her face up with new pancake makeup that came in style. She looked so beautiful. Nobody could believe it was her! Mama made ten-year-old "Baby" Kaye a blue lace dress to wear to the wedding, with material from what was once an old gown.

Now, the Accardos were beginning to go "high tech," relatively speaking. They could finally afford a telephone. Of course, it came with a three-way "party line." If you picked up the phone to place a call, and someone from one of the other two connections was already on the line, tough luck. You had to wait until they were finished. If you interrupted too much, they might get mad. If it was an emergency, you could state so loudly and clearly. Only then would the party line participants hang up and allow you to use the phone immediately. Those were the rules, plain and simple. None of it was written down or mandated. The party line culture, and its rules, barely kept pace with the explosion in technology. Yet for the most part, no one complained about it. Of course, no one knew that soon a telephone line of your own would be available at a reasonable price. This new, extra modern form of communications transfixed the imaginations of Vauxhall and changed lives. What was there to complain about?

For many families, including the Accardos, the end of the Depression meant that music came into their lives in ways never before imagined. Now, they were able to afford new radios. Each afternoon at 5:00 p.m., Charlie Barnett's hit song, "Make Believe Ballroom," or Clyde McCoy's "The Sugar Blues," could be heard playing loud and clear on almost every radio on Montclair Avenue, blending with the smell of fresh "gravy." Record players were added to the repertoire of pleasure items. It wouldn't be long before small, vinyl "45" records, about seven inches in circumference, played hit songs at a speed of forty-five rounds per minute. The forty-fives were stacked one atop another on a round tube that dropped them down the turnstile one at a time. It was modern miracle. Now, the girls could practice their dance steps with ease, especially to the smash jitterbug hit, "In the Mood," my favorite song, by the Glenn Miller Orchestra.

As the Depression melted away, everything seemed to be getting better and better all the time in America, and certainly in Vauxhall. At Bamberger's, a huge Christmas Dinner and Dance was planned. It would be held at the famous Essex House in Newark. Bamberger's made sure the event was a smash hit. They hired Harry James and his orchestra to play in the upstairs main ballroom of the Essex House. Downstairs, another band, led by one of Bamberger's own former employees, a one-time elevator operator named Johnny Jackson, played. It was too much fun for one night. The guests, including me and my sister, Jeanette, ran upstairs and downstairs to dance until the wee hours of the morning.

Grandma Nana's house, next door, was a second home for the Accardo children, literally. Since the Accardos upstairs apartment was beginning to get crowded with five grown children, for a while during the Depression brother Nick had to sleep next door at Nana's. Jeanette and I took turns sleeping with Aunt Kaye at Nana's, our "second mother" next door. But the Depression was over now. The children were pretty much fully grown, all having graduated from Union High School. So Papa decided it was no longer necessary to rent the apartment on the first floor of the house on Montclair Avenue. Finally, with the Depression a fading memory, the Accardos were once again able to reclaim full control of our house for the first time in nearly a decade. Once again, the Accardos had a living room, a dining room, a kitchen, two bathrooms, and all the bedrooms upstairs. The upstairs kitchen remained in service as well, providing extra capacity. For the most part, it was used for ironing or other activities that had been compressed into the more limited space. Few families had enough money to fully remodel. For the Accardos, the extra space was good enough.

During the Depression, New York City seemed a distant place from northeast New Jersey. It was expensive to get there and expensive once you arrived. So trips to New York were limited. Yet as the Depression concluded, New York City became much more than just a view from nearby South Mountain for the Accardos. Now, it was a place to take the family for special occasions. Mama would take the grandchildren by bus from Union to Radio City Music Hall. A big treat was to go to the new-wave food automat, Horn and Hardart, the art-deco, glass-and-chrome cafeteria-like establishment. There, you could view and then select the food of your choice, through miniature glass windows, and pay through a coin-operated system. You would insert the proper amount of coins and a tray of food would spring out. It all seemed so modern, so perfect once again. The Accardos had gone from rags to riches in America. The Great Depression forced them back from riches to rags. Now, finally, they were going back to "riches" again. Nothing could slow their new momentum this time. Or so it seemed. And then came Adolph Hitler.

1. Cover: Photo of "Papa."

2. Mama dressed in her finest in 1916, one year before her wedding to Papa.

3. Mama and Papa on their wedding day, July 1, 1917. Their marriage was more than a product of love at first sight. It was arranged by relatives.

4. Mama and Papa show off a fig tree in the yard of their home in Vauxhall, New Jersey, in 1930. True to their Sicilian farming heritage, the Accardos were fairly self-sufficient when it came to food.

5. The Accardo family Christmas tree in 1944. With a son and two son-in-laws off to war in World War II, Papa at first would not permit a celebration, much less a Christmas tree. He relented when his daughters suggested a tree with American flags instead of ornaments and pictures of their U.S. Army loved ones placed beneath.

6. Papa proudly displays the American flag raised on his three-story wood-framed house in the Italian section of Union, New Jersey, in 1943.

7. Mama pregnant with Mary in 1921 (From left to right.) Mama, Nana, Aunt Kaye Deo, an unknown individual, Jeanette, and Nick.

8. Mama and Papa cut the cake at their fiftieth wedding anniversary.

9. Mary (center) with cousin Nunzio Manfre, from Latina, Italy, and his wife Vincenza, on a trip by the Manfres in 1987 to visit family in the United States.

10. Papa at the age of eighty-one at a family celebration.

11. Papa at his ninety-third birthday party with his five children (left to right) Mary Militano-Winters, Anna Petruzziello (seated), Jeanette Castagno, "Baby" Kaye Scarpa, and Nick Accardo.

12. Papa examining a homegrown squash raised in the garden to his broth-
er-in-law, Uncle Pete Deo. Papa never stopped appreciating good
farming.

13. Mary dancing with Papa on his one hundredth birthday.

14. Mary shares a loving moment with Papa.

Chapter III
The War Years

In the late 1930s and early 1940s, Papa had a good job as a house painter and decorator. It was hard work. Papa would return home from a long day in a thoroughly exhausted state. After supper and a glass of wine, he would put his head in his hands and rest for about fifteen minutes. Then he would be back at work again, tending to the garden in the summer or fixing shoes in the basement in the winter. Painting was a labor of love for Papa. He enjoyed the work and would teach the Accardo children how to paint and wallpaper with style. It was good work. And good work was supposed to be hard. So it was part of life, pushing forward to make ends meet in America.

Papa's boss, Mr. Waller, was of German decent. This was nothing unusual in Union, which had a large German-American population. Along with the Italians, Irish, Jews, and African-Americans, the Germans contributed to a colorful and diverse town. Mr. Waller would come by the house from time to time on Montclair Avenue, spend a few hours, and would soon settle onto the bench at the stand-up piano against the wall in the living room. The Accardo children would be delighted when he played one of his favorite songs, "The Star Spangled Banner."

Yet there was an ironic undercurrent to it all. Mr. Waller, it seems, had befriended members of a new and emerging political party in Germany, one with American affiliates in the United States. And it was not entirely clear what this new political party meant to America, if anything. Mr. Waller's friends would attend meetings of the new party and would occasionally try to explain what it stood for.

Much of it seemed odd to the Accardos. There was something peculiar about it all, beyond the general disinterest Mama and Papa had for politics. Yet Papa couldn't put his finger on what was so odd. Even the name of this new German political party sounded odd: the Nazi party.

Since the fascists in Italy had found common cause with the Nazis in Germany, Mr. Waller felt comfortable talking with Papa about the Nazis. Mr. Waller's friends would attend pro-Nazi German-American Bund Meetings in Chicago. One day, they asked Papa if he would like to travel to Chicago to attend one such meeting. Mr. Waller obviously didn't know Papa very well at all. Papa had a gut sense for his new world. He knew a good thing, and a bad thing, when he saw it. He had an inherent sense of right from wrong. He had already resisted La Cosa Nostra, which was much closer to home than this Nazi party in terms of his family. Papa would have none of this Nazi party stuff. It was all nonsense to him. Besides, there was far too much work to be done to sit in political meetings. Who had the time for such a thing? For Papa, it was nothing doing.

As war broke out more forcefully across Europe, and the true intentions of the Nazis to build the Third Reich became brutally clear, things turned sour pretty fast for Mr. Waller. He was arrested. Uncle Ben, by then a successful lawyer, represented him in court. But it was of no use. Mr. Waller was dispatched to a detention camp in the southern part of the United States, where he sat out the rest of the war. More than likely, living in America meant that Mr. Waller had little idea of what the Nazis across Europe truly planned. In the aftermath of the war, he was vindicated.

Since everything was measured in personal terms in the Italian enclave of Vauxhall, World War II had not yet struck home in the earliest days of the 1940s. Word of the arrest, and incarceration, of Mr. Waller would echo through the neighborhood and then pass. There were no twenty-four-hour news channels to keep people up-to-the-minute on world events. People had to try a lot harder to access the news. And the inhabitants of Vauxhall had too little information, and too much work to do, to worry about the crisis descending over Europe.

World War II newsreels were tagged on to popular movies in theaters. Radio journalism had begun, but not everybody had radios. Few of the families purchased newspapers on a daily basis. As Adolph Hitler was grabbing power in Europe with brutal force in the late

1930s, the schools in Union were focused more on ancient history than current events, which you were supposed to learn outside the school system. Prior to America's entry, the war was still considered a somewhat remote and distant thing in Vauxhall, especially for the Accardos. If anything, they worried more about their relatives in Sicily then their own fate at home. To compound the information vacuum, the Accardo family rarely discussed politics in the house, much less world events. Not much else was going to penetrate the steady, ongoing drum-beat focus of trying to successfully raise a growing family in a new country, with all of the work that went along with it.

All of that began to change on December 7, 1941. With the Japanese attack on Pearl Harbor, it didn't take very long before World War II became very real indeed to the inhabitants of Vauxhall. Something cataclysmic had occurred to all of America. And it was about to get personal. As their own family members were inducted into military service, what had been "Europe's war"—World War II—had arrived on the steps of 267 Montclair Avenue. Son Nick, son-in-law Joe, and soon-to-be son-in-law Johnny were drafted into the United States Army. The Accardos were now learning about the war from a newly-purchased radio, or the newspaper, which they had begun to purchase on a regular basis. Papa would relate the current events in the United States to what he was reading in mail sent by the relatives back home in the old country, Sicily. He learned from family that much of Italy had turned communist and fascist. People were scared. Even going to church had become a source of suspicion. In a bastion of Roman Catholicism, the Sicilians had grown intimated doing something that was deeply ingrained in their culture...going to church.

One by one, as the men began to go off to war, and the reports from the relatives in Italy grew increasingly dire, the reality that Vauxhall had indeed been sucked into a global conflict were now very apparent indeed. In a short period of time, the level of interest in World War II among the Accardos went from distant to hitting right at home.

Life in America, and for the Accardos, was beginning to change in other ways at the onset of world war. For me, life was about to become far more complex and interesting. Just a few blocks away from the house on Montclair Avenue, in the town of Maplewood, the Militano family resided on Springfield Avenue. Like the Accardos, the Militanos were a proud Italian family of direct Sicilian heritage. Frank Militano, the father, was a barber in town. The mother, Emanuella, tended to the family. The Militanos had eight children: Tina, Sam, Frank, who was called "Babe," Nancy, Rose, Anna, Tommy, and Joe. Of them all, Joe was a particularly handsome young man, with piercing blue eyes, wavy blond hair, a distinct Roman nose, and a warm smile that would melt the house away. Only "Babe" shared the blond-haired, blue-eyed good looks in the Militano family. Yet there was something about Joe's graceful style that seemed to brighten whatever environment he inhabited. So it didn't take me very long to catch his eyes, and apparently, vice versa.

While I took a "special" interest in Joe, Mama had her own plans: she invited the Militanos over for dinner. Mama suddenly tossed out family information that was brand-new to me: apparently, Joe's parents had attended Mama's and Papa's wedding. This was important information, indeed! After all, it meant that the Militanos were much more than just another family down the block. They were Sicilian. *And they were family friends!* One Sunday, Mama made a ton of raviolis, a special treat, with fantastic gravy. Papa made his homemade wine. As the Militanos arrived for dinner, both sets of parents knew exactly what they were doing. The signal could not have been more distinct or clear: They were tacitly giving their blessing to a union of the families, a union, after all, between Joe and me.

A Wartime Wedding

As my nineteenth birthday approached, the air was filled with anticipation, some good, some mixed with concern. On the one hand, a romance was in full bloom. Now Joe was my fiancé. He gave me a fantastic cedar chest as a gift, an appropriate gesture given the expectations that had been set. Together, we would fill the chest. Mama got the ball rolling. One item she placed inside was a beautiful, sky blue, organdy bed cover with pillow shams. Another was a set of white Miniver Rose towels with huge large red roses sewn on.

Mama invited Joe and his family to the Accardo house for my birthday. Yet there was something peculiar about Mama that day, and

I couldn't quite put my finger on what it was. Joe and his family were to come by the house for coffee, cake, and of course, wine. Mama had baked a cake and delicious cream puffs. Yet when I arrived home from work, Mama was sick in bed. Something had come over Mama, and no one could figure out what it was. Sadly, Mama had suffered a miscarriage. Yet, amazingly, no one, except Papa, even knew she was pregnant! In her true pioneering spirit, Mama soldiered on. She fought to not let it slow her down, or for anyone to see. She endured it like a steady ship full sail in a storm. She weathered it, and kept it to herself and Papa. Mama wasn't about to let a family birthday pass without a celebration, especially one that would include the two new lovebirds. With the accumulated strain taking its toll, and with the birthday preparations almost complete, Mama would remain in bed for several days, physically, and emotionally, drained.

At relatively tender ages, Joe at twenty-four, and me at twenty-one, the two lovers were ready to get married. But there was a war going on. Papa had a fit at the very thought of the two of us getting married, considering the circumstances. Quite specifically, Papa was afraid that Joe wouldn't come home from the war. Then, I would be widowed, which could be emotionally and socially crippling in Vauxhall. There was the possibility that marriage would never come my way again. Marrying Joe was simply out of the question. Papa refused to recognize the thought. He demanded that we put off our plans. When we said we wanted to marry anyway, Papa threatened to put a stop to it in the most fundamental Sicilian male way he could think of: He would refuse to walk me down the aisle.

Yet Mama wasn't quite so hard over. She knew a romance when she saw one. Her own marriage had been arranged. So she was determined that her girls would marry the men they fell in love with. What did it matter that a war was going on? Life could not grind to a screeching halt. Mama told me to just give it a little time. Papa would come around sooner or later. She told us to begin to plan our wedding. Which is exactly what we did.

For Papa, more than a little convincing was in order. It was bad enough that Joe was most probably going off to war. On top of that, it was unseemly during times of war to excessively celebrate. Papa could not conceive just what type of wedding this would be after all. Waiting until after the war was over seemed far more logical to him.

Yet romance and momentum were moving just as fast as the soldiers were heading off to war. Papa saw nothing left to do but relent. There were conditions, however. Papa was promised that we would have a quiet, dignified wedding that didn't denigrate the times, in which America was at war. We arranged to have a simple turkey dinner at a local restaurant, the Club Royale, on Stuyvesant Avenue in Union. A small band was hired for dancing. It was a relatively modest event, in distinct contrast to the typical Sicilian-American weddings of the time, which were huge feasts with hundreds of people, and partying and dancing that would go on well into the night. For $3.95 per person, Joe and I were married in a simple ceremony and reception. That's not to say we didn't have excitement. The Crystal Bakery forgot to deliver the wedding cake. No worries. The Union Police Department was sent to the bakery where the proprietor's home telephone number was posted on the door in the event of such "emergencies." The police called the baker. He came out to the store, unlocked the door, and delivered the wedding cake. Nothing was going to stop us now.

Uncle Tony Fontana, Papa's only blood relative in America—his first cousin—approved of the new marriage in his own way. Few of the Vauxhall Sicilians used whipped cream at the time, since it was very expensive. Instead, a very sugary icing was placed on top of cakes. Apparently, the icing at the wedding was so sugary that many of the guests couldn't eat it. So Uncle Tony did the right thing. The lingering effects of a Depression-era mind set still existed. There could be no waste, *ever*. So Uncle Tony did what he had to do. He collected everyone's unused icing, piled it high in his plate, and polished it off fork-by-fork until he was ill. Our wedding had been blessed, on behalf of Papa's family back in the old country, by the loveable, and nauseous, Uncle Tony Fontana.

Off with the U.S. Army to North Carolina

As the war broke out even wider, and spanned four continents, Joe was drafted into the United States Army. Private First Class Joseph Militano was assigned to the 100th Infantry Division, one of ninety Army divisions. The 100th was activated on our wedding day, November 15, 1942. At first, Joe was shipped off to Fort Jackson, South Carolina. Then, for additional training, he was shipped to Fort

Bragg, North Carolina. With sheer determination, I was never too far behind. The Army wasn't about to slow this romance down, at least not just yet. To the contrary, I took a leave of absence from my secretarial job at Bamberger's and applied for unemployment benefits in North Carolina. The Jersey girl was now taking control of the situation.

As newlyweds, we rented a room in a multiple-family dwelling next to a funeral parlor near Fort Bragg. The owner, a woman named Gladys, made cash renting rooms to soldiers and their wives, or girlfriends, when they visited. Joe and I had kitchen privileges. We could cook inside to save money, since the Army pay and unemployment didn't amount to much. So I loaded a few supplies in the kitchen and opened up for business. Soon after, it was a mystery why so much red wine vinegar was missing from the kitchen. Even if someone had borrowed a little bit, there was no way it should run out so rapidly. Then the landlord, Gladys, and the men from the Funeral Parlor, were spotted chugging the vinegar! Apparently, old Gladys had a bit of a drinking problem. One theory was that she thought the vinegar would kill the smell of hard booze on her breath, which wouldn't be appropriate for a proper Southern landlord. Another was that she simply thought the vinegar got her drunk.

During the daytime, the men would be out of bed at 5 a.m. to catch the bus to Ft. Bragg. The visiting wives could take a bus trip to the lake, go shopping, or take one of the sewing classes that the Army had arranged for us to pass the time. Or, we could just grab a blanket, lie out in the hot Southern summer sun, and catch a tan.

Evenings were much more lively. The boys would be back from the base at night and looking for action. Most nights were spent at the Ray Avenue USO. There, a great Army orchestra would blare away till the wee hours of the morning. It was pure fun. Joe and I were especially good dancers. We would tear up the dance floor doing the ubiquitous jitter bug. The huge Ray Avenue USO hall was filled with hundreds of soldiers, their wives or dates, and a number of Southern girls looking for single GIs. Occasionally, another soldier would ask Joe's permission to dance with me, and Joe would oblige the fellow, but just once. As the Gershwin's tune "Embraceable You" wafted through the air, Joe and I fell deeper in love. "Embraceable You" would be *our* song, our theme song, for years to come. Away from home for the first time, we were finally together. The world had come to a full stop. The war would have to wait. Romance was in the air.

My overriding goal was to create a slice of New Jersey in the deep south. One day, I shopped for the ingredients to make spaghetti sauce in a North Carolina supermarket near Fort Bragg. This wasn't so easy. Ingredients for Italian food, as simple as pasta sauce, or "gravy," were not so readily available. Yet I was determined to make sure that Joe had a little taste of New Jersey whenever he wanted it, at least while I was with him in North Carolina. So I improvised. A little of this, a little of that. Maybe it didn't taste as great as back home, but it was the best I could do. If Joe didn't like it, you would never know. He wasn't fussy and it wasn't his style to complain about anything, much less dinner with his bride.

The Militanos soon grew tired of living in Gladys's house near the funeral parlor. Gladys said I had a New Jersey accent. I said Gladys had a Southern accent. I told Gladys that a library nearby once housed slaves. Gladys would deny it, apparently out of pride. Worse, there were mice in the apartment, which Gladys didn't believe. My worst fears came true one day when I discovered that a table cloth, which had spaghetti sauce spilled on it, was nibbled away. Now I had to sleep with the covers pulled over my head!

Joe learned of an opportunity to share an apartment with another solider and his wife, the Livingstons. So the two couples moved in together. Soon, the Livingstons were being treated to my home cooked gravy, with spaghetti and meatballs. John Livingston wasn't about to miss an opportunity to enjoy a good meal. He liked certain things a certain way and he wouldn't be denied. He simply poured ketchup over the top of the pasta, blended it with my pasta gravy, and made a concoction of his own.

Life was certainly different in the south than in New Jersey. The pace was more laidback. And the relationship between black people and white people was notably different. Segregation was in full force in the south. The black folks were not allowed inside movie theaters along with the whites. As I walked through the streets, I was shocked to see black people jumping off sidewalks to let me pass by. While plenty of racism existed up north, it wasn't so obvious. This simply wasn't something you would see in New Jersey, even if racism up north had its own manifestations.

Yet the Carolina moon had had its desired affect on us after all. The two months alone in North Carolina had brought the newlywed couple much closer together, in more ways than one. The warm, sultry southern sun, and evenings dancing wildly to Army bands, intoxicated us with romance. With Joe's opening tour of duty winding down in North Carolina, I went home to Vauxhall as he shipped off to Europe.

As Joe boarded an Army transport ship bound for Europe, I boarded a train back to Vauxhall. Both of us were bluer than blue. All of the fun in North Carolina was now a recent memory. Joe would shove off to some far-off land. The war could not wait. Yet there would be no guarantees of Joe's return. Maybe he would come home safely. Maybe he wouldn't. Yet, for us, a miracle had occurred. Soon after I returned to Vauxhall, I learned that I was pregnant. A baby was on the way! I was ecstatic. Mama was, too. I loved the thought of being pregnant with Joe's baby as my husband went off to war. In a most earnest way, I didn't want to see him go off to war, in harm's way with only a ring and a piece of paper to bond us together. Now, we were truly a family, married and with a child on the way.

Yet there were at least two people in the world who would not be so happy with this so-called "good news": my boss at Bamberger's... and Papa. This was exactly what Papa was afraid of. It's why he didn't want me to marry Joe at the time in the first place, instead of waiting until the end of the war. At first, Mama didn't even want to tell Papa that I was pregnant. She figured that could wait until my pregnancy grew more obvious. We could buy some time to figure out how to drop the bombshell. Having returned from North Carolina, Papa kept asking me when I planned to go back to work. Mama and I knew we were shoveling sand against an inevitable tide. The moment of truth would soon be upon us.

The Caissons Go Rolling

As life moved forward for Mama and Papa and the girls in Vauxhall, son Nick, and sons-in-law Joe and Johnny, were scattered around the globe with the U.S. Army. Often, there was no telling exactly where they were. Mail was censored and often the location of the troops was secret, especially if they were planning an attack. Brother Nick wrote one letter with the opening, "Dear Melba," and wanted to know about his friend "Sydney." These were clues! Melbourne and Sydney are cities in Australia. Nick was in Australia! Soon, he would ship out to India and China. Yet, the U.S. government worked hard to ensure a degree of continuity. Nick was with the U.S. Army Signal Corps in China when I was married. He packaged and mailed a beautiful antique Chinese bowl as a wedding gift. After dinner, Papa would always ask if there was any mail from Joe, who went from France into Germany with the Army. Joe's mail was censored too, with entire sections cut out. However, mail from Joe would arrive once per week, at a steady, reassuring pace.

By now American pop culture had moved into a melancholy, wartime mood. Film and music reflected the ache that swelled inside so many hearts back home and around the world. A most popular song was the painful lament, "I'll Be Seeing You," which underscored the sense of war-time separation. *Since You Went Away*, starring Claudete Colbert, Shirley Temple, Lionel Barrymore, and Agnes Moorhead, filled the movie theaters. Bob Hope brought a slice of America to the homesick troops around the world. Nearly all of his radio shows during World War II were broadcast live from the war zones with American troops.

There was a small record player upstairs in the Montclair Avenue house. Before going off to Europe, when Joe was home on furlough, together we bought the record *Paper Doll*. We played it over and over again until it was ringing in our ears. For me, it would bring back recent memories of happy times. Papa would hear the song playing when he came home from work, and would ask if Joe had written recently.

Mama enjoyed the patriotic American war songs, especially the songs recirculated from World War I. "Over There," or the traditional "Battle Hymn of the Republic." With one son and two sons-in-law in the military, the songs made Mama proud of her Sicilian-American family's contributions to America. Still, she couldn't resist rearranging some of the words for sporadic comedy: "Glory, glory hallelujah, my teacher hit me with the ruler. Mother hit me with the broomstick and made me black and blue."

During the war years, the trolley cars had virtually disappeared from Springfield Avenue in Vauxhall. The new, modern buses took over on the main thoroughfares. Yet few new buses hit the streets, if any, during the war years. Industry was no longer focused on making cars and buses. Instead, the American "Arsenal of Democracy" was churning out equipment for the war effort: vehicles, aircraft, ships, ammunition, and supplies. The factories were humming. With a fewer number of buses in service, every bus along Springfield Avenue now bristled with people. Sometimes it was impossible to get a ride. Yet no one ever complained. This was a generation that had endured a Great Depression. Now they would win a world war. Complaining was not a part of their vocabulary.

When Christmas rolled around, Mama and Papa said it wouldn't be right to put up a Christmas tree. Brother Nick was now in India. Joe was in France. Anna's fiancé, Johnny, was in the Pacific Theater. How could the family put up a Christmas tree when three family members were in harm's way? Yet the girls had a better idea. We couldn't skip Christmas altogether. The men at war wouldn't have wanted us to be so dour. So Mama and Papa agreed to put up a small tree with lights only, but not ornaments. Instead, we would decorate the tree with small American flags. We placed the pictures of our loved ones in service, dressed in their uniforms, under the tree, out of respect. With their Sicilian sons now defending the U.S.A. at war, in the truest sense of all, the Accardos had now fully become Americans.

A Telegram to Germany Heralds a New Arrival

As the 100th Infantry Division of the United States Army penetrated deeper and deeper into Germany in 1945, Joe was among the troops. From a Militano family perspective, events were unfolding in Vauxhall almost as fast. I was in labor. But no one had a car handy. And the pains were getting worse. Soon, it became apparent that action had to be taken. Never mind a car. We called a taxi. Joe's mother, Emanuella, and Mama, remained with me at the hospital. Then, shortly after 5:00 a.m. on May 16, 1945, while Joe was living in a captured castle in Germany, a baby boy was born. "It's a boy!" Papa was crazed with excitement! Who cares whether he was originally on board with this marriage or not. This was the first boy born into the Accardo family in twenty- seven years! Papa was thrilled. Mama sent Joe a telegram with the announcement. The soldiers with Joe scooted around the castle and scoured to find a few bottles of champagne. Suddenly, an impromptu celebration ensued. Joe mailed back a picture of himself at a desk, holding the telegram. A baby had been born to the Accardo family of Vauxhall, New Jersey. And the father was nearly five thousand miles away at war in Germany.

I wanted to name the boy "Joe Jr." after Joe. However, Joe wanted the boy to be called "Richard." With a war going on, and Joe in harm's way, this was a small amenity he could have. So "Richard" he was. Baby Richard would get all of the attention that any child could ever want. He had at least three "mothers," instead of one. All in one house along with me were Mama, grandma Nana, who came to live with us after their house next door was sold, and my sisters. U.S. forces were beginning to roll through Germany. A baby boy was born in Vauxhall, New Jersey. And for one Sicilian-American family, the two events would be forever entwined.

As World War II dragged into its fifth year, the Maplewood movie theatre, near the house on Montclair Avenue, was by now showing newsclips of the conflict in earnest. The war had become the all-consuming topic of conversation in Vauxhall. "Where are the boys?" "Have you heard from any of them?" "When do they think it will end?" Movie-goers were shown newsreels from the "RKO Pathe News." Listeners could tune into *The March of Times* on radio. The movie reels became a primary source of quality information, with great black and white visuals, bringing home a conflict so geographically far away. Radio could provide live accounts, with legends such as Edward R. Murrow broadcasting live from the rooftops of London during the "Battle of Britain" to the final days of the Third Reich.

It all seemed to be barreling to a close. Then, on May 8, 1945, the war in Europe was over. Celebrations broke out in the streets from Vauxhall to Times Square. The good news was broadcast by radio. "Extra, extra" echoed through the streets of Vauxhall as newspapers spread the cheer. "VE" day, "Victory in Europe," had finally arrived. Three months later, on August 15, 1945, "VJ" day, for "Victory in Japan," was celebrated. For the Accardos, there was an especially wonderful aspect to all of this and great cause for personal joy and satisfaction. All of the men of the Accardo clan would come home safely to Vauxhall. The war was over. And God had blessed the Accardo-family servicemen.

With a brilliant chant, a neighbor, Frank Venezia, bellowed the blessed words: "Joe is getting off the trolley at the end of the street!" on Montclair Avenue. He was early. Baby Richard was hurriedly dressed. I raced to the foot of the steps, baby in arms. The front door swung open. And there he was! Dressed in a dapper U.S. Army uniform, my solider had returned home, to me, safely. He clutched the baby in his arms and beamed a radiating smile, as the women sobbed uncontrollably.

Soon, Mama and Papa would be surrounded by all of their children again, their sons-in-law, their daughter-in-law, and their grandchildren. It was a time of great joy and anticipation. Mama celebrated by doing what she did best: She made mountains of raviolis! Hundreds would be made for Sundays. Mama would buy dough from the nearby Italian bread store to make Sicilian pizza. Papa wanted his with anchovies. The children would have none of that, opting for the more traditional tomato sauce and mozzarella, with sausage on top. Mama and Papa could never be sure who would come for dinner. With Mama's great cooking and Papa's "fine" wine, they could be sure of one thing only: they would never be lonely on Sunday afternoons.

For the returning servicemen heroes, it was a monumental transition. From foxholes to Sunday dinners at Mama's and Papa's, everything about them had dramatically changed for the better. The women loved seeing their men in uniforms. But the men couldn't wait to buy new suits, sick and tired of putting on the same old uniform, day-in and day-out. They didn't want to be reminded, anyway, about the war they had just come back from. For many World War II veterans, returning to civilian life meant leaving the war-time memories behind. Anna's husband, Johnny, saw hair-raising action as a paratrooper in the South Pacific with the Army's 11th Airborne Division. Instead, the men preferred to focus on the good stuff now, their brides, and in some cases, their babies. They would go to Howards in Newark to pick up a flashy suit for $24.95. Then they would go dancing!

The Accardo family, and their growing extended family, had endured more than most could imagine. Their roots included a journey from an old country to escape economic decay and fear. They had somehow navigated the straits of the Great Depression and emerged stronger than ever. And now the greatest war in the history of the world was over and all of their sons would come home safe.

The "GI Bill of Rights," government loans and massive development projects, made it relatively easy for the returning servicemen and their wives to purchase new homes. For nearly all, it would be their first house. An aerial photo of Union, New Jersey in *Life Magazine* depicted a complex of 350 small homes, just a few miles from Vauxhall. The complex was expressly developed to accommodate the veterans who had returned home from the war. It was a perfect development for Joe and me. So what if the house had only four first-floor rooms, an unfinished attic and unfinished basement? After all that our young family had endured—from the Great Depression through a World War—the house was a slice of heaven. The basement could be finished, someday, as a recreation room. Extra bedrooms could be built upstairs. With no time to waste, we purchased our first home for $11,900 at 175 Locust Drive in Union. We packed up and moved in with our son, Richard, and our beautiful new baby daughter, Mary Jane.

By the mid 1950s, the average annual salary in Union was about $3,000. It was enough for us to afford the most modern of all inventions and amenities, the television. There were five channels to select from, all emanating from New York City. Programs such as *Ozzie and Harriet*, *I Love Lucy*, *Gunsmoke* and *Lassie* became instant favorites. Kicking back and watching TV in the post-war years underscored our triumph and newfound prosperity. At long last, the extended Accardo family's topsy-turvy Sicilian-American dream appeared to be heading in the right direction once again. This time, perhaps, for good.

Chapter IV
Selling the House at
267 Montclair Avenue

Being of Sicilian decent in America carries a special meaning if the roots of the Old World remain freshly connected to the vine of the New World. Having *famiglia* in Sicily made that all very real in human terms. With "blood relatives" in Sicily, the circle was complete. Mama always sent the relatives clothing, even in later years. When one of Papa's nieces was getting married, Mama bought the entire bridal outfit and sent it over.

Papa made a point of staying connected. His sister, Vincenza, remained in Sicily even though Papa emigrated to the United States. With the war fading in their collective memories, and the fear associated with travel to Europe now fully dissipated, in August, 1953, Papa decided it was finally time to go back home, for the first time since he stepped foot in America. Some thirty-seven years after he arrived at the gates of Ellis Island, Papa would finally go back to Sicily. He would return by ship. And he would be fully prepared: since there was no indoor plumbing back at the homes of his family in Sicily, and you couldn't be sure of the sanitary conditions, he brought his own toilet paper...just in case.

By then, all of the Accardo children were married with children, with too many bills and not enough time to go with Papa to Sicily. Mama felt it was more important to remain behind to help the family at home. So Jeanette, her husband, Anthony, Baby Kay, and Mama went to see Papa off from New York harbor. For the first time since he arrived in the New World, Papa set sail for the Old World.

Of course everyone in the Accardo clan in Vauxhall missed Papa. He was a quiet and unassuming man, yet the void created by his absence was enormous. Papa was that sweet source of comfort, stability, and fun that was an expected staple of our lives. And now he was missing from the day-to-day life of the Accardos at 267 Montclair Avenue. Worse, visiting the family in Sicily was not a weekend excursion or a two-week vacation. A trip to see the family was accorded all the formalities, and pleasantries, of a royal visit. There were too many people to see, and too many places to go, so you certainly couldn't rush the visit. No, this couldn't be a two-week visit. There could be no hard-and-fast schedule. You arrived, and later returned home, only after you had seen everyone you needed to see. And after thirty-seven years in America, loaded with tons of stories about the new world, which the relatives had to hear first-hand, Papa had a lot of people to see. He remained in Sicily for more than three months.

To Papa, Sicily really hadn't changed very much. Unlike all of the development in America, in the rebuilding years following World War II, Sicily was still very much a farmland, with few modern amenities. Papa, now a modern "American," returned as an example of the growth and relative prosperity that the United States had afforded this Sicilian immigrant from Gibellina. Papa enjoyed making the rounds. The relatives treated him like a rock star. He had achieved one of the most enviable heights of life's accomplishments: He left a poor Sicilian farmer, and now he was a "wealthy" American with an indoor bathroom, plumbing, and a television!

Finally, the family back home in Vauxhall began to play at Papa's heartstrings. After two months had passed, we wrote him a letter describing the autumn leaves turning the color of burnt orange and red in New Jersey, with a fresh chill in the air. All of us missed Papa sorely and told him so. The holidays were approaching. Even if the Sicilians thought the holidays began the week before Christmas, in America the holidays started one month earlier, at Thanksgiving. Surely, Papa couldn't miss Thanksgiving. To think of all the stories he could tell the family about life in the Old Country. Papa returned to America on November 18, 1953, just in time for America's celebration of nation and family. Besides, he couldn't have stayed much longer in Sicily...his toilet paper had long run out.

The Sicilian relatives would soon be just as mobile. A massive earthquake erupted in Sicily more than a decade later and leveled Gibellina, Papa's place of birth. The town was entirely destroyed. The few remaining eighteenth century structures that survived were knocked down nonetheless. A great labyrinth, the Labyrinth of Gibellina, was created in place of the original location, tracing the streets of the original town that once existed there, in a concrete maze. The town itself, and its inhabitants, were relocated some twenty miles away.

Papa's sister, Vincenza, did not appreciate the idea of recreating a home town that had been flattened. It wouldn't be the same. She would not try to recreate Gibellina twenty miles away from her birthplace. It just didn't seem right. The Italian government was providing assistance for the evacuees to relocate, to find an apartment and to purchase clothing. It was time for something new. Papa's mother and father had long since died, so there was nothing keeping the family in Sicily, where jobs remained scarce, the volcanoes were threatening, and the Mafia had crept into everyday life. If Papa could emigrate all the way to America, surely Vincenza could find someplace new. So she and her family used the money from the Italian government to relocate about ten miles south of Rome, in the little town of Latina, near the Mediterranean Sea.

Visiting family now became a two-way-street. Papa's nephew, Nunzio, who lived in Latina, would soon represent his greater Sicilian family on visits to America. Once, he brought a bag of snails, which he raised in his yard in Latina, as a gift. Papa put them in a pan on top of a radiator, to keep them warm in advance of an escargot dinner. Yet the snails had ideas of their own. They climbed out of the pan, up the walls, and were going for the great escape. No matter, it didn't take long for the grandchildren to hunt them down and bring their prey back to the kitchen where they belonged.

Nunzio was amazed at the relative level of wealth that his family had achieved in the United States. It wasn't just the nice houses and clothes, or the fact that most of the families had automobiles. It was the extended wealth across all of America that was so stunning to him. Compared to earthquake ravaged Sicily, or the war-damaged areas around Rome, America was prospering at levels never before experienced. Supermarkets were a particular source of amazement.

How could the Americans eat sausage in the summer months, Nunzio asked, when the inevitable bacteria could regenerate and create an inedible product. Sausage was something you ate only in the *winter* in Sicily. After all, these biologically combustible animal parts had been melded together inside stomach lining shaped like a tube. The notion of refrigeration and owning a freezer had not yet sunk in with Nunzio. The summer would rot the sausage, wouldn't it?

The two-way street of transatlantic visits now became part of the Accardo family tradition. With Joe, and good friends, Betty and Jack Mageean, we visited Papa's sister at Nunzio's home in Latina. As Vincenza waited at the gate of her home, I approached in a white pantsuit, improper for an Italian woman, yet common in America. To my older Sicilian aunt, I was now a symbol of the modern American female, outspoken and confident, and with a fresh new expression of freedom in dress alone. The relatives swarmed to see their American family and friends. Joe and Jack, both firefighters, were taken for a tour of the local fire station in Latina and were greeted by an honor guard, saluting and standing at attention. After years of neglect, our Italian language skills, spoken so fluently in the Accardo home years before, had grown rusty. An Italian-American dictionary, forever by our sides, helped us bridge the language gap. Yet beyond language, there was no gap at all when we visited the relative in Latina. These were *familgia*. There was no emotional distance. 4,300 miles, an ocean and two continents were erased with a simple smile and a warm embrace.

Sunday Dinner, Still, at Mama's and Papa's

By the mid-1950s, the Accardo clan had grown immensely. Nick had two daughters, Marguerite and Diane. Jeanette had two daughters, Janet and Nina. Joe and I had three children, Richard, Mary Jane, and Joseph. Anna had three children, Maryann, Vincent, and Johnny. And "Baby" Kaye had three daughters, Susan, Karen, and Vicky. So now there could be as many as twenty-five mouths to feed at the Accardos on Sunday for dinner after church. Nothing could make Mama and Papa happier than a packed house. While the size of the dinner party might vary, some things remained exactly the same. Mama would continue to make the cherished raviolis, the children's favorite, as the volumes grew and grew. Papa continued to make his beloved homemade wine.

These were special times. Cultural traditions were passed direct-ly down through two generations. Each grandchild, assuming they could hold their own glass, would get a shot glass of red wine. It was good for them. It was good for their blood. It made them relax. It was no different decades earlier when Papa would give the older grand-children, Richard and Maryann, a sip of wine as they watched him squeeze grapes while they played in the basement. Mama would spot their purple lips and holler at Papa.

Now comfortable in their retirement, Mama and Papa built their lives around helping their children and grandchildren. It never struck them to pack up and move to Florida, for the warmer weather, as many American retirees did. They stayed where they were needed, with their children and grandchildren. Raising a family had always been their ultimate purpose in life, and that was not about to change in their senior years. Helping their children aspire to greater prosper-ity, and enjoying all of the remaining years together, continued to be the focus of Mama's and Papa's senior years. It was the Sicilian way. If one of the children was setting up a new house or apartment, Mama would bring linens. Papa would arrive with his favorite paint-brush and roller in his hands. In a single glance, he could tell if an eight-foot-long section of wallpaper was crooked. If so, he would remove it and paste it back correctly. There was never any doubt about babysitters. The question was whether one of the daughters, or Nick, would ask first. Either way, no problem. On any given Saturday night, blends of grandchildren from each of the families could be found with Mama and Papa. If any of the family members paid for a babysitter, it was an insult.

As the years progressed, the house at 267 Montclair Avenue seemed to physically grow in size as Mama and Papa grew older. Caring for the house had become difficult. It was simply too large for them after all the children had departed. So, reluctantly, Mama and Papa concluded it was time to sell. The bittersweet realities of an entire life were beginning to take hold of them. They had conquered a new world, a Great Depression, and survived a war. Yet they could not, ultimately, outlast the human experience. After all, old age had come to Mama and Papa.

Jeanette's husband, Anthony Castagno, a police chief in nearby Bloomfield, New Jersey, located an apartment for Mama and Papa across town in Union, nearby Anna's house and not far from mine and Joe's. A Shop Rite supermarket on Morris Avenue was within walking distance, so they could be self-sufficient food-wise from day-to-day. Together, Jimmy and Lena Accardo would now swing open their folding shopping cart, push it a few blocks, load it with food, and wait to see who would show up for Sunday dinner. Yet now they had competition for the attention of their grandchildren. America had taken a bite. Now, Little League games, neighborhood barbecues, and car rides on the Garden State Parkway to the Jersey Shore would compete. Yet Sundays would invariably still bring company. The lure of pasta and homemade wine could not fully dissipate. Perhaps the amount of mouths to feed around the table would be fewer. Still, they would come. Life continued to be sweet, in America, for Mama and Papa.

The Brittle Realities of Life

One day, Papa was painting a two-story house in Union. In many respects, it was dangerous work, which included climbing steep ladders to the peaks of the houses. Yet it had to be done. It was Papa's job. And if it was his job, Papa would do it efficiently and safely. He simply learned to be careful. There was little choice.

For those who made their livelihood on scaffolding decades ago, living on the edge is more than a figure of speech. It was a constant balance of pulleys, ropes, and shifting weight. There was a feel to it all, much like fishing in a small boat. One day, the scaffolding Papa was working on suddenly swayed. Stress built in the ropes. An eerie sound pitched through the air. Then, with little warning, the ropes snapped in two. The scaffolding disappeared beneath Papa's feet. His partner grabbed the side of the house and held on for dear life. Sadly, Papa was not so lucky. He was thrown more than twenty feet to the ground.

Papa was rushed to a hospital in the nearby city of Elizabeth, New Jersey. Joe and I scrambled to get to the hospital. Papa was badly banged up and covered in paint. He was in agony. Yet he was alive! He hit the ground and slammed on the side of his body, with a broken hip. A nurse provided the name and telephone number of the surgeon who was scheduled to operate the next day. As much as we wanted to help ease the pain, there was little we could do for Papa. If we even considered one of the homespun medical methods to ease his pain, the surgeon had sober advice for us: "If you don't know what to do, do nothing." But doing nothing was not the Accardo family style. There had to be something we could do. At the hospital store, I purchased a child's book, the Little Golden Book version of *The Night before Christmas*, ultimately destined for baby Richard. Yet the book would first be loaned to a senior gentleman in great pain. Its first stop would be Papa's hospital room. Still a kid at heart, Papa didn't let the fact that it was child's book get in the way of his rehabilitation process. He needed something to lift his spirits. And nothing could lift his spirits better than Christmas. There, with a broken hip, a smile drew across Papa's face, as he read *The Night before Christmas*.

Of course, Mama visited Papa in the hospital. Joe and I drove her there during a furious snow storm. Perhaps we were unaware of an old Italian superstition: "Bad things happen in threes." With Papa lying in a bed upstairs in the hospital, Mama made her way through the parking lot toward the building. Ice and snow covered the walk. Mama plowed ahead. Suddenly, she tripped. As she fell, Joe grabbed her by the arm, twisted around, and fell on top of her. His one hundred seventy-five pound frame crushed down on Mama. A snap was heard. Now, Mama was in the emergency room with a broken arm. It was unwise to tell Papa. It would upset him and there was no need. He could find out later. With Mama in one room of the hospital, and Papa in another, two of three bad things had occurred. It was a harbinger of what would come next.

Parkinson's Disease has a tendency to sneak up on its victim. One day, they feel fine, the next day they don't. No one at first seems to understand what is wrong. At the time that Mama was first diagnosed with Parkinson's, it didn't seem so threatening. The medical community had recently discovered the "wonder drug" L'Dopa. The medicine visibly helped Mama. Her hands stopped trembling and she was able to continue to write checks to pay the bills. She could still shop for groceries and do the cooking, which she loved so dearly. The cooking in particular was what made Mama, Mama. It was more than her role. It was her never-ending gift to her family. She was a fabulous Italian cook. Best of all, Papa, her children, and her grandchildren associated her cooking with the finest tastes that they had ever experienced. Nothing was better than Mama's cooking!

Yet Mama would often tire of taking her pills. She would stop for days at a time. She felt good. So why swallow pills? This couldn't be a way of life, taking pills all the time. The dependency alone was anomalous to such an immigrant survivor's mentality. Unfortunately, Mama had no idea what danger she created for herself by having lapses. One day, while taking a break from the pills, Mama fell down. Papa managed to get her into bed. I came by immediately and contacted the family surgeon, Dr. Alan Jacobs. He asked if Mama's left foot, on the side she had fallen, was pointed outward. It was. Mama had broken her hip. An ambulance arrived to transport Mama to Overlook Hospital in Summit, two towns away. The doctors set her hip in surgery.

On her second day after surgery, Mama seemed to feel somewhat better. A nurse, not knowing that in addition to the hip fracture, Mama also was a Parkinson's patient, told her to exercise by walking with a walker. It was far too early for such exercise, especially for a Parkinson's patient. Fate was about to strike once again. Tragically, Mama fell a second time, breaking the hip a second time. The doctors were unable to operate once again so soon. Parkinson's Disease and two hip fractures took their toll on Mama. She went directly from Overlook Hospital to a nursing home in West Orange, New Jersey. Soon, she was suffering from senility as well.

Mama could be taken home for holidays, but Papa realized just how unfair it must be to send her back. None of it was fair. Yet it was life playing out to its natural conclusion. On July 24, 1980, at the age of eighty-four, Mama passed away. By then, she and Papa had lived apart for some time. His conviction to remain by her side in every emotional way possible never once faltered. He would visit her often. He suffered in his own way when Mama was taken from him by a dreaded disease and two falls. Of course, he dearly missed having her with him. Since the day when he first saw her, peering through the door of Nanu's house, and he knew she was the woman he wanted to marry, they had raised five children and sixteen grandchildren. They had lived a full life together, more full than most, and certainly grander then either could have imagined. At the age of ninety-three, Papa soldiered on, with Mama forever in his heart, and his family by his side.

Before Mama got ill and passed away, in many ways their lives had come full circle. They had brought a touch of Sicily to America. Their Sicilian-American family had grown and was flourishing. Their grandchildren would come by to visit.

When Mama and Papa had been married fifty years, the children decided to have a wonderful celebration for them. It would begin with a renewal of their wedding vows at St. Joseph's Church in Maplewood, New Jersey. In many ways, it was a spiritual renewal for the entire family. Nephew George Deo served as the organist. The summer sun was brilliant. It radiated the intense love and affection fifty years of marriage had created. After church, the party quickly shifted to the Town and Campus hotel and restaurant in Union. There was a large hall, the Alban Room, decorated in gold décor, which was perfect for their "Golden Anniversary." Mama's and Papa's bridal party attended, including Mama's sister, Kaye, who was a "junior" bridesmaid, and her brothers Sam and Ben, who were ushers. Uncle Tony Fontana represented Papa's family. The grandchildren were all seated together at one very long table. Pictures of fifty years of love adorned the room. Two large posters depicted Mama's and Papa's life together.

The Town and Campus had selected a wonderful band for the occasion. Yet Papa still wanted his friend, Mr. Louie, to bring his musical group to play all of the Italian favorites. After all, Mr. Louie had serenaded the Accardo family on special occasions so many times before. Above all else, this was a celebration of family and friends. So Mr. Louie's band of merry musicians had to play. The children hopped around the dance floor to the Sicilian favorites.

Mama's and Papa's fiftieth wedding anniversary would be the first of two such celebrations that would bring the Accardo-Romano Sicilian-American experience full circle. It would be a joyous event. Lena and Jimmy Accardo danced to the Anniversary Waltz. It would be the sweetest of sweet celebrations. Yet it would be the last time that Lena and Jimmy Accardo would dance together in such a magical moment. It would be a capstone of their Sicilian-American journey. Their next great dance would have to wait, until they would meet again on another dance floor, in a place even greater than America.

A Centenarian Named Jimmy Accardo

Immediately after Mama's death, Papa, at the age of ninety-three, lived with each child for a month or two. Yet, this arrangement surely wouldn't work forever. It was a nice way for Papa to remain directly connected to each family member, to spend time with the children and grandchildren. Yet sooner or later, Papa needed a sense of permanence. Anna, the "Little Angel," took him in to live with her in Union. The sisters pitched in when Anna and her husband, Johnny, would go on vacation or to Atlantic City.

Papa had his quirks. If he couldn't sleep during the night, Anna could hear him counting up to one hundred in Italian. The joke was that, since he didn't have any money, no one could guess what Papa was counting. After a lifetime in America, he was still getting used to the New World. One day, Papa picked up an electric shaver instead of his usual razor, brush, and shaving cup. All was well, until Johnny went upstairs and found Papa dipping the electric shaver into the shaving cream.

Papa would continue to enjoy the small things in life after Mama's death. Even in his nineties, he would putter around the garden and grow vegetables. He would take walks in the wooded area behind our house with our dog, Rocky. He would sit on a chair in the yard and keep watch over a large brown rabbit that would approach. He would pass the time playing cards, even if no one else was around, playing solitaire by himself. Papa was an inherently happy man, who needed very little to amuse him.

With the age of one hundred years approaching, Papa still had wavy grey hair. He could still walk to the barber one mile away. He still loved good food and a glass of wine during every lunch and dinner. And he continued to smoke a pipe or an occasional cigar. If his longevity defied a set of odds of their own, his emigration and endurance through a Great Depression, and two world wars, made it even more remarkable. Papa would offer one piece of advice to anyone who asked how he lived so long, in such a healthy state. "Moderation," he would say. "Do everything in moderation."

On his one hundredth birthday, on August 30, 1987, Papa's American hometown newspaper, the Union Leader, declared it "Jimmy

Accardo Day" in Union. He was the oldest living man in the township's history. A wall plaque was presented by the Union Township Committee. Of course, the occasion demanded a huge Sicilian family celebration! It would be conducted at the local hall of the Union Council of the Knights of Columbus, the Roman Catholic fraternal organization. Among the 135 guests were Nunzio, Papa's nephew, and his wife Vincenza, who came from Italy to represent the relatives. Vincenza baked wonderful Italian cookies and brought them to America for the party. Father Derbyshire said a special mass for the family immediately before the Saturday party so everyone could sleep in on Sunday morning. Papa's five children brought up the offerings at mass. Everyone could feel Mama's presence. When her name was raised, it was filled with joy, and a tear blended in.

Finally, Jimmy Accardo, the one-hundred-year-old immigrant Sicilian, now an American and centenarian, rose to the floor...and danced. In one small step, he had achieved all the dreams and aspirations of a generation. Jimmy Accardo of Gibellina, Sicily, was an American now, and he was the man of the hour in his American hometown.

Where Did All Our Family Go?

A certain expansion and contraction sometimes occurs in the lives of immigrant American families. As the first generation arrives in the New World, they flourish and grow in numbers as their families enlarge, per ethnic custom. Yet ethnic traditions of raising large families in America, while passed on, in many cases were unceremoniously passed up by subsequent generations. Families grew and grew until the original members were far outnumbered by grandchildren and great-grandchildren. Yet as the American Baby Boom generation conceived fewer children per family, the trend began to reverse itself. For the immigrant patriarchs and matriarchs, who survived to see it all, sometimes a new reality emerged. Their families, and extended families, were *shrinking*. As he continued to live beyond his one hundredth birthday, such was the case for Papa. Most of his contemporaries had died. So had many friends and family members who were much younger. As the Accardo family got smaller and smaller through the years, one could only ask: "Where did all our family go?"

After Papa's one hundredth birthday, each new birthday called for celebrations of their own. The old Sicilian who moved to America continued to outlast all odds. It was as though he was possessed. Having witnessed the most remarkable transformations of all—from houses without plumbing or bathrooms in Sicily, to his fellow Americans landing a man on the moon—there was still much more to see. He had one bad eye. He needed a second new set of false teeth. And he detested the bunions that would grow on his feet. Otherwise, Papa was the picture of health, physically and emotionally. On his 101st, 102nd, 103rd, 104th and 105th birthdays, Jimmy Accardo would again make the front page of the *Union Leader*. With so many contemporaries dying before him, each year he would receive his plaque from the Union Town Council, and the day would be commemorated in his honor. The children, grandchildren and now even great-grandchildren, would gather to celebrate a life, a culture and lineage, all wrapped up in one. Papa's birthdays, until his death of old age just before his 106th birthday, were far more than birthday celebrations. They were celebrations of tradition, of family, and of overcoming the odds. They were celebrations of ethnicity passed on to thirteen grandchildren and fourteen great-grandchildren. They were celebrations, indeed, of Sicilian-Americanism, a place and time where the Old World, once again, met the New.

Such was the legacy that Jimmy Accardo, "Papa," left his family when he died simply of old age on October 9, 1992. Even in death, the extension of his family continued. He had brought a slice of Sicily to America, where it would remain forever. One grandchild, Mary Jane, was in the Ukraine with her husband, Mike, seeking to adopt a baby. When she learned of Papa's death, she began to sob uncontrollably. Moved by witnessing her emotions, the man in charge of the orphanage expedited the procedure and honored the couple with a four-month-old son, John Michael, in perfect health.

At the hospital where Papa passed away, the doctors wanted to do an autopsy to see what made the old guy tick. Yet the family somehow knew that an autopsy would not tell the full, or real, story of Jimmy Accardo. An autopsy would offer little explanation of Papa's longevity. His was a more complex story than pure physiology. Of course Jimmy Accardo had great genes and was a hearty physical specimen. But he ate, drank and smoked as he pleased. The real story of Jimmy Accardo was not so much about genes or physical prowess. The real story was about overcoming the odds, about not sweating the small stuff, about grieving the inevitable loss of family and friends quickly and moving on. The real story of Jimmy Accardo was about living life to the fullest. It was about loving your family and friends, about never forgetting where you came from, and always appreciating where you lived.

When Father Derbyshire eulogized Papa, he said that God had given Jimmy Accardo the grace of a long and healthy life. While many came to McCracken's Funeral Home in Union to pay their last respects, Papa had outlived all of his contemporaries, especially Mama. Jimmy Accardo had beaten the odds, more than once. His emigration from Sicily in 1916, and unpredictable personal triumphs in America through two wars and a Great Depression, had defied chance. For one last time, Papa made the front page of his hometown newspaper, the *Union Leader*. It was his century, a Sicilian-American's century, and Jimmy Accardo had made the most of every minute of it.

Epilogue

Quite often, I dream of Mama. The matriarch of the Accardo family more easily seeps into my subconscious. Yet my most fervent wish is to one day dance with my papa again at one more Sicilian wedding. When we were very young, each evening before we fell asleep, in the silence of the night, we would call out to Mama and Papa, as we were taught: "Sa Beneditto Mama, Sa Beneditto Papa. God Bless you." And then we would await their reply, "Santo et Ricco. Be Blessed and Be Rich."

Mama and Papa have their names listed on "The American Immigrant Wall of Honor" at Ellis Island for posterity. When Ellis Island was renovated, Papa was asked to represent the Sicilian immigrants at a ceremony. Yet, Mama's and Papa's legacy is far more rich than names on walls. Today, a Sicilian-American family with roots in the Old World is forever in touch with their ethnicity. Jimmy and Lena Accardo remain alive today in the celebrations of seafood and pasta at the grandchildren's homes on Christmas Eve. You can see them alive, still, in the eyes of the great-grandchildren as their faces light up on Christmas morning. You could sense they are still here when the men of the family, who, no matter their profession, can work the garden or fry a meatball. You can find Jimmy Accardo in the handy pocket knife that he once carried, which today is entrusted to his grandson, Vinny, or his favorite pocket watch in the hands of his grandson, Richard. You could sense the presence of Mama and Papa when Nunzio's wife, Vincenza, weeps at the appearance of her American relatives visiting Latina generations later. In the Accardo family, they cry when you arrive, they laugh and feast in the middle, and they cry when you leave.

Most of all, you can feel the presence of Jimmy and Lena Accardo in the love of children, of famiglia, of music and food, in finding pure joy in the smallest things in life, of never sweating the small stuff, and always celebrating what you have. Jimmy and Lena Accardo took big gulps of pleasure from the cup of life to the very last drop. And because of that, they will live forever.